SpeakEasy Magazine: FREIRAUM – Phase 2

ISBN 978 1 9163881 5 4

Copyright on all materials in this magazine remains the property of the individual contributors.

Cover Artwork: Jill Pemberton

Artwork Photographed by: Francesca Halfacree

Cover Design: Philip Hewitson

First Published in the UK in 2022 by Caldew Press.

Caldew Press
Tolivar
12 St George's Crescent
Carlisle
CA3 9NL

Please send a cheque for £10.00 each, plus £2.00 post and packing (UK).

Caldew Press email: caldew-press@outlook.com

Special thanks to Francesca Halfacree, Jill Pemberton, Jack, Sam, Tom, Lily and Adele Pemberton, The Pemberton family.

Thanks to Dr Jane Dudman for curating Phase 2 of Freiraum UK, Prism Arts, Matthew Wallace at the Methodist Central Hall, Jilly Jarman, Geoff Bartholomew, BlueJam Arts, Linda Fitzgerald and Shireen Hama.

Also the Goethe-Institut for instigating Freiraum, and ArtBOX Thessaloniki for project coordination. And Keith Partridge, Ed Cooper, David Robert of the University of Cumbria for making magic happen.

Finally thanks to:

Aftab Khan for curating Phase 1 of Freiraum UK and enabling us to create a sphere of freedom.

Susan Cartwright-Smith for her tremendous work on *SpeakEasy Magazine: Freiraum* (2018).

Becca Roberts for her support, enthusiastic nature and enduring wisdom.

Many of the following works were incorporated into the *SpeakEasy meets Freiraum* film which premiered on YouTube on 31st October 2020. The order of some work has been rearranged for this collection.

Thank you to all the contributors, every one of the writers, poets, artists, musicians, singers, photographers and filmmakers, who found extraordinary ways to express feeling, emotion and communication in our free space, a safe space, this sphere of freedom, our Freiraum.

SpeakEasy Magazine:
FREIRAUM – PHASE 2

Editors:
Philip Hewitson, Susan Cartwright-Smith

Contributors:
Nick Pemberton, John Charlesworth, Josephine Dickinson,
Stephen J. C. Hymers, Kelly Davis, Janette Ostle, Barbara Renel,
Ally Barr, Lou Rodger, Fernando Smith, Tony Hendry,
Harry Cartwright-Smith, Clare Louise Roberts, James Scott Riddick,
Juliet Fossey, David Simmons, Ros Edwards, Valerie Moody,
James Ovens, Craig Davidson, Carolyn Richardson, Ben Naga,
Marc Robinson, Kevin O'Connor, Chris Reed, Peter Robinson,
Becca Roberts, Susan Cartwright-Smith, Philip Hewitson,
John Chambers, Nicola Reed, Andy Hopkins, Laura Rutter,
Jill Pemberton
and
Shireen Hama, Linda Fitzgerald,
Jilly Jarman, Geoff Bartholomew,
Dr Jane Dudman.

Published by Caldew Press 2022

Johannes Ebert, Director General of the Goethe-Institut, is presented with the first copy of *SpeakEasy Magazine: Freiraum* by Susan Cartwright-Smith and Philip Hewitson at the SpeakEasy Freiraum special event of 9th December 2018.

Freiraum in Carlisle 'Making our Sphere of Freedom'

A short film showcasing the UK's involvement in Goethe-Institut's Freiraum project.

CONTENTS

'Freiraum' artwork – Jill Pemberton	i
Presentation to Mr Ebert (photograph) – Tolivar Productions	iv
Summer – Carolyn Richardson	x
The splendid isolation of the artist...	1
SpeakEasy poster 25th April 2018 – Philip Hewitson	2
Notes on isolation – Nick Pemberton	3
SpeakEasy Freiraum special event 9th December 2018 – Various	4
Without you there's nothing to do...	5
Photographs – Tolivar Productions	6
Manifesto – Dr Jane Dudman and partners	8
Improvisation with BlueJam Arts – Jilly Jarman, Geoff Bartholomew	9
In honour of child refugees – Shireen Hama	10
Star – Linda Fitzgerald	11
SpeakEasy meets Freiraum poster – Philip Hewitson	12
Mission statement – Philip Hewitson	13
Illustrations and 'A response...' – John Charlesworth	14
The gift – Josephine Dickinson	24
Not flocking, following (22 March 2020) – Janette Ostle	25
When time stopped (The Richardson Street Blues) – S J C Hymers	26
Conversation with my father – Kelly Davis	27

Trapped inside the tower – Lou Rodger   28

Without you there's nothing to do – Harry Cartwright-Smith   29

This is not a poem about the coronavirus – Clare Louise Roberts   30

Let's hew – James Scott Riddick   33

Umwelt – Fernando Smith   34

A journey with no plan, no idea...   35

One step at a time – Valerie Moody   36

Everywhere – John Chambers   37

Photograph – Craig Davidson   37

Lockdown poem – Peter Robinson   38

Photograph – Craig Davidson   38

'Lockdown' artwork – Marc Robinson   40

'Coming out of lockdown' artwork – Marc Robinson   41

Easter Sunday morning, Wigton (12 April 2020) – Janette Ostle   42

Catalan cowls – Fernando Smith   44

Elsewhere... something happens – James Scott Riddick   45

'Self portrait', 'Don't look back', 'Cloud', 'Solway sun' artworks – Kevin O'Connor   46

Borderlines – Ally Barr   48

Together apart – Valerie Moody   49

Artwork – Janette Ostle   51

And we painted rainbows – Philip Hewitson   52

Intercontinental tea – Ally Barr   53

Photograph – Craig Davidson	54
I ate the whole cake – David Simmons	55
Artwork – Janette Ostle	56
Poem as role handover – James Scott Riddick	57
Walton Moss – Chris Reed	59
Territory – Ally Barr	60
Photograph – Craig Davidson	60
The tragedy of the peacock prince – Ros Edwards	61
Parakeets in the park – Tony Hendry	63
The ants of Lisbon – Fernando Smith	64
Poem from the future: The trees lead the way out of the gorge – Juliet Fossey	65
Artwork – Janette Ostle	66
Spiral down – Susan Cartwright-Smith	67
Towards Mockerkin – Craig Davidson	68
Between the lines – Barbara Renel	70
Resonance – Josephine Dickinson	71
Photographs – Craig Davidson	73

How far will hope stretch... 75

We are clay – Ally Barr	76
In the whirlwind – James Ovens	78
Me – Ally Barr	79
The magic of words – Ben Naga	80

Baby's best heels – Fernando Smith	81
A new light – Valerie Moody	82
How far will hope stretch – James Scott Riddick	83
Second wave – Kevin O'Connor	84
The centre of the world where we will meet – Fernando Smith	85
Drifter – Clare Louise Roberts	88
Lullaby – Harry Cartwright-Smith	90
Breathe in water – Susan Cartwright-Smith	91
The night we almost said goodbye – Nicola Reed, Nick Pemberton, John Chambers	92

Find yourself a key... 93

Artwork – Janette Ostle	94
True to you – Philip Hewitson	95
Interview excerpt – Becca Roberts	96
Cross country – Tony Hendry	97
Artwork for 'Lavender' – Laura Rutter	98
Lavender – Nicola Reed, John Chambers, Andy Hopkins	99
The mad accordion – Nick Pemberton	100
'Stormy seas' photographs – Craig Davidson	103
'Some words on Isolation and Freedom' – SpeakEasy	104
Acknowledgements	105

Biographies	106
'Freiraum' artwork – Jill Pemberton	110

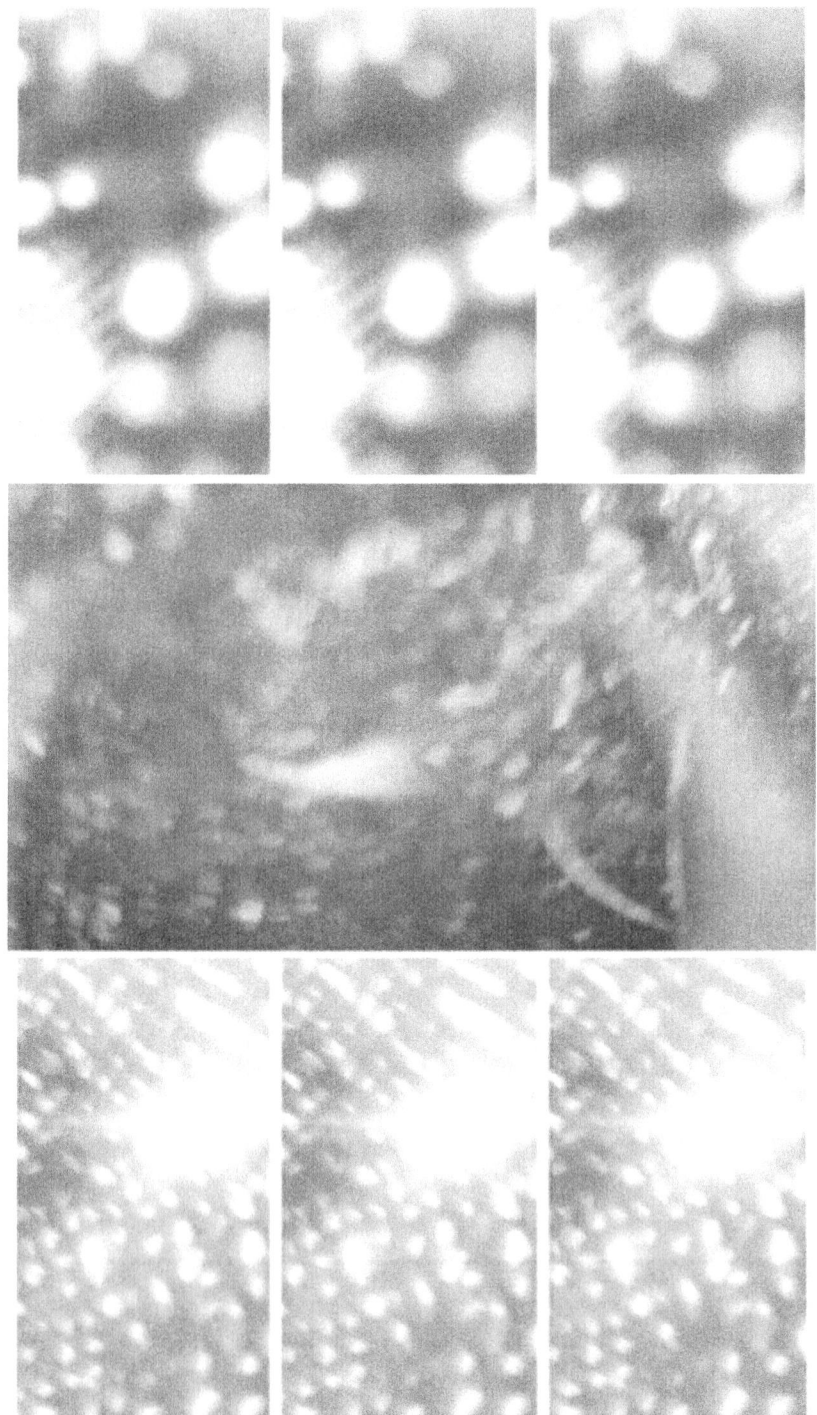

Summer
Carolyn Richardson

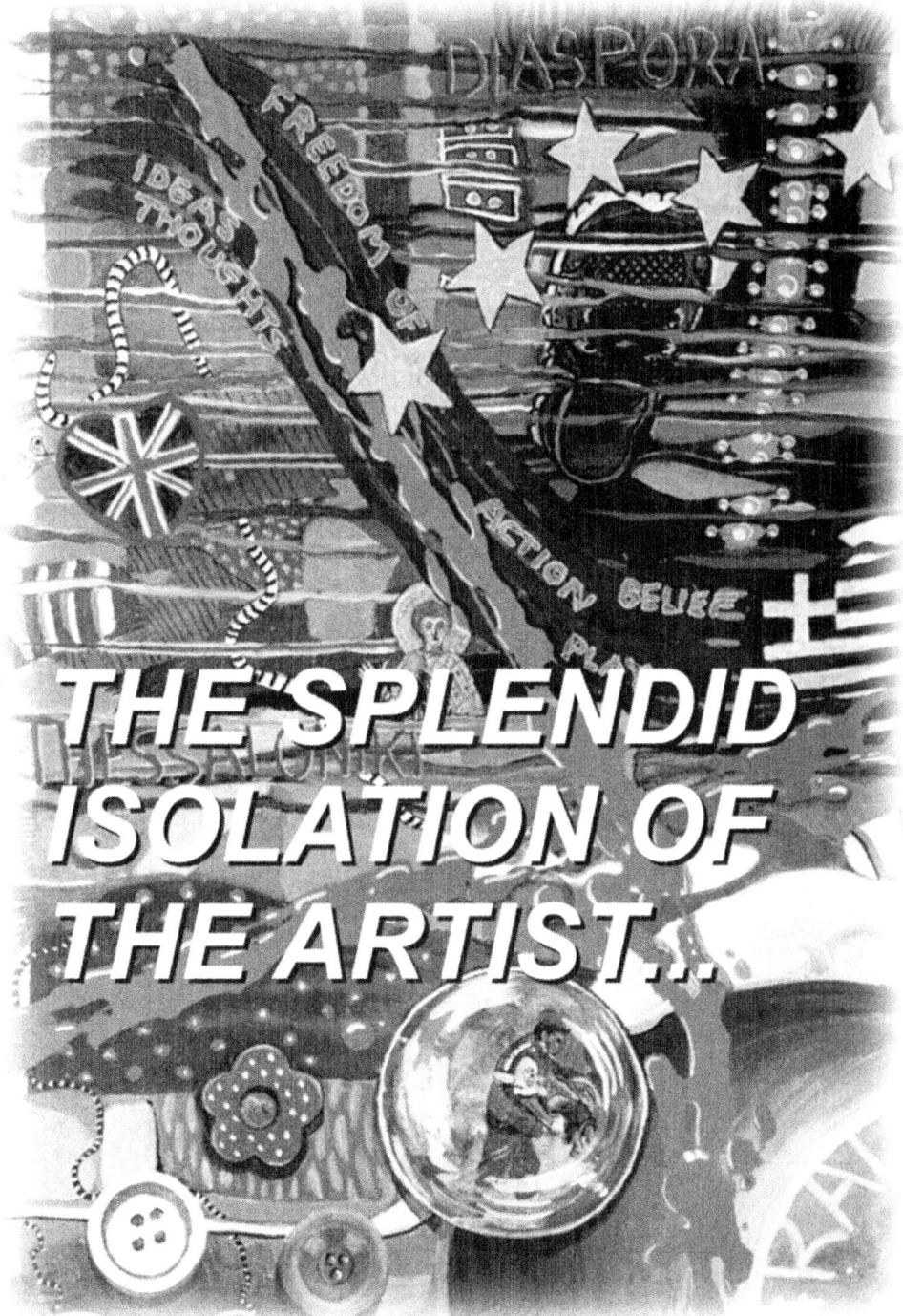

Notes on Isolation
Nick Pemberton

Isolation through indifference

Isolation as a disconnect and a state of disconnectedness

The splendid isolation of the artist

The splendid isolation of the prophet without honour in his own country

Isolation through anger, through disgust, through a rebellious nature

Isolation through time, through ageing, through changes

Isolation from families and lived out through families

Isolation through lack of the required skill sets -language, numeracy, education

Isolation through love -for whatever reason- ending

Isolation through shyness, through difference through -is this the right word- disability?

Isolation through abuse, physical, mental or substance (and they're all connected)

Isolation as a self imposed state of being

Isolation as exile -often internal

The isolation that comes from living without limits, from not knowing where you stop and someone else begins

The less than splendid isolation of someone who is so far up themselves that they haven't noticed that everyone else has begun to isolate them

The isolation of the single mum, the long distance dad, and anyone anywhere who has lived without being loved

And -might as well steal a last line- we gazed upon the chimes of freedom flashing.

Event programme produced by Susan Cartwright-Smith

CARLISLE FREIRAUM
SCHEDULE
REGISTRATION: 1.30PM
PART I: 2.30PM – 3.45PM

Welcoming address from **Aftab Khan**, Development Manager, AWAZ Cumbria
Opening by **Councillor Liz Mallinson**, Chairman of Cumbria County Council
Guest Speakers:
Johannes Ebert, secretary general Goethe Institut
Cristos Savvidis, ArtBox, Thessaloniki – *Freiraum* Carlisle – Thessaloniki Link,
Speakeasy Notes by **Nick Pemberton** – read by **Phil Hewitson**

ISOLATION & OVERCOMING ISOLATION

What is Isolation by John Charlesworth – read by John Chambers
Poetry – by Crystali Glyniadaki
Concerning a funeral – Mick Yates
A pin to soften the lock – Annika Browa
Poem – Amjad Alassad
Music performance by BlueJam Arts
The Language of my Bones - Deborah Beckett
The woman who walked into Doors - Hazel Stewart
Everything must change – song – John Chambers
Dear Rosie – Lou Rodger
Poem – Shireen Heme
Poem – Linda Fitzgerald
Thoughts on Isolation – Alison Barr
Isolation in Carlisle – Adrienne Gill
Freiraum – Susan CS
Poem – Mohammad Taha read by Amjad Alassad
Breathing Space – James Riddick
Notes on Isolation by Nick Pemberton – read by Andy Hopkins

WWW.GOETHE.DE WWW.ARTBOX.GR

CARLISLE FREIRAUM
SCHEDULE
PART II: 4PM – 5.15PM

FREEDOM

Link up to Thessaloniki – 30 minute exchange
Poets: Phoebe Gianissi, Vassilis Amanatadis, Mario Chatziprokopiou
Sphere of Freedom – Philip Hewitson
Uffaq-e-Azadi – Aftab Khan
'Alphabetula' - Josephine Dickinson
(Video) *poem* - Katrin Joost
Music - John Chambers, Nicola Reed and accompanying *video* by Laura Rutter
Between the lines – Barbara Renel
Dabbin Houses by nightjars – (Andy Hopkins, Nicci Reed and John Chambers)
The Tiny Boy who lives on my Record - Mollie Nixon
Freiraum – Marilyn Messenger
The pied piper in prison – Calum Taylor
A Question of Forever – SJC Hymers
(video) *Song* by Ruth E. Cockburn
Mind Tree – Jean Hill
Locked in the Cabinet – Hannah Borlase
What is Freedom by John Charlesworth – read by Susan Cartwright-Smith

CALDEW-PRESS@OUTLOOK.COM

CARLISLE FREIRAUM
SCHEDULE
PART III: 5.30PM – 6.30PM

EUROPEAN IDENTITY (WHO ARE WE, WHERE ARE WE, WHO ARE WE WHERE WE ARE)

22:22 Montemaitre Paris – Katie Evans
No future No England Dreaming – Fernando Smith
Unthanks – Andy Hopkins
Icarus – Savannah Evans
EU – John Grieve read by James Riddick
In Lyon - Tony Hendry – read by Ruby Evans
Love is – Nick Robinson read by Annie Kendall
Recasting – Ruby Evans
Whinlatter – Annie Kendall
Reading - Melanie and Cristina
Refuge – Ben Naga
Woman goes for Solitary walk – Jane Moss-Luffrum
This Parlish Land – Susan CS
Facebook response – Nick Pemberton read by John Chambers
Performance/closing remarks - Johannes Ebert
View from the 155 bus – Philip Hewitson
(video clip) – Nick Pemberton, Kelly Davis and Becca Roberts

WWW.TOLIVARPRODUCTIONS.COM

SpeakEasy Freiraum special event, 9th December 2018
Brampton Road Arts Campus, University of Cumbria

Carlisle in lockdown during the COVID-19 pandemic...

Carlisle in lockdown, 17th April and 4th May 2020.

Freiraum Manifesto

Dr Jane Dudman and
Freiraum partners

FREIRAUM: TO ALIGN UTOPIA AND PRAXIS

1. Freiraum is a space for Freedom: a space for one to feel safe, angry, critical, accepted, included, respected and empowered.

2. Freiraum is also a tool-kit of practices, and a network of actors and places, creating new narratives and alternative futures.

3. To be free demands greater responsibility than to be oppressed: it requires action.

Valorising difference to fight indifference

4. Freiraum is not singular but multiple, and it continuously strives to be presented, articulated and disseminated as such.

5. We strive towards a space that invites and enables people to be themselves, through a diversity of pragmatic, actionable down to earth approaches.

6. Freiraum is a call to the silent and for the silenced to become audible.

7. Freiraum announces its presence through calls to be more visible and to actively participate in public life in the squares, the streets and everywhere people exist politically.

8. Freiraum acknowledges the importance of the message, and the historical prominence of the 'billboard' as a place where the story of the world is advertised.

9. In order to go beyond superficial change-making, Freiraum brings content, imagination and political thinking back to the billboard.

A culture of reflection and learning

10. Freiraum asks: How can we learn from each other and do small things with great impact? Who can be, and who is dissident now?

11. How do we align utopia and praxis, prioritise freedom before necessity, organise the idea, organise the revolt?

12. In search of answers, Freiraum strives to make a step ahead, through transgression, diversion, shared responsibility and subversion.

We want to transform silence and whisper into informed public speech and action.

Improvisation with BlueJam Arts
Jilly Jarman and Geoff Bartholomew

Jilly Jarman and Geoff Bartholomew are an improvising duo of jazz pianist/vocalist and trumpeter who play live with sampled, found sounds and effects.

In Honour of Child Refugees

Shireen Hama

Small faces, fearful, confused faces, weak bodies, badly broken hearts, an uncertain future.
Strange people around them.
This is what I saw in the pictures.
I know the world was rough with them.
How painful the war was, how difficult it was to escape, how long the journey was, and how unknown the future was for them.
I felt for a moment that what happened several years ago may repeat with us now.
Displaced people... afraid... it does not matter if the reason is the same, what matters is that the stories are the same.
History repeats itself. Fear returned victorious over us and over them.
Death was the first to knock on their doors.
Loss was their first visitor.
Loneliness was the story of the lives.
Some say that the children are lucky to be able to forget, their memory is not as strong as an adult's strength.
I don't think so!
I asked myself... Is the sound of fear and death still in their dreams as it is in my dreams until this day?
Will a hospital bed really heal their wounds?
Can the temperature of the room warm the cold in their hearts?
I don't think so!
Yes, we can live and reach great numbers of ages in life, but do we really want to live this long?
Or do we hope for death every moment that we cannot call our parents?
Do we really have goals and dreams, or were our dreams just to call our parents every time we fall on the floor for help?
Do we really want a doctor or a kiss on our forehead before we sleep?
Do I have the same features of my mother or father's face?
As a lost child in a strange and difficult world... everything I want is the sweet that my father bought me.
I want my brother to play with me.
In this harsh world we will find people who help us and people who understand us, but will we find people who feel what we feel?
Maybe yes, but the question here is... who these people are?
They're just the same people who went through what we went through.
What I want to say is...
The memories never leave us.
They come every day as a dream, or in a word or in a view, or as a thought.

Star

A child's face is a bright star
It glows and shimmers
Like sunlight on water.
In some young lives
Darkness can come
Terrifying shadows
Cold & bitter confusion
That star-light dims.
It becomes only a faint
Glimmer at the back
Almost invisible.
What you need to do
Is fix on that spot and
Stay with it, don't let it go.
Undertake activities to disperse
The black clouds of fear, of pain...
Progress may be slow
You need to give it time
You may not see any kindling
In the present season or the next.
The sprinkle and sparkle of the
Star-face though, will return.

They are not 'they'.
A young life needs a light to
dance
under and they need
you to give it to
them.

L.F.

Star
Linda Fitzgerald

Speak easy
Meets
FREIRAUM: PHASE 2

**Overcoming Isolation and celebrating creativity in a FREE SPACE by sharing Poetry, Spoken Word, Music, Art, Film, Life
31st October 2020**

MISSION STATEMENT

SPEAKEASY meets FREIRAUM: PHASE 2

An event will be taking place on 31st October 2020 as part of the Goethe-Institut's latest phase of the 'Freiraum' (Free Space/Sphere of Freedom) project.

Amongst various online talks and discussions across Europe about social and cultural freedoms, and ways creativity has survived in a time of COVID-19 and what the future might hold for the Artistic Community, is the opportunity to take part in a Festival of Freiraum.

A special SpeakEasy event will be taking place as part of Freiraum events once again in Carlisle. We will be one of several events taking place on Saturday 31st October 2020 (time TBC).

Arrangements are still being made but this may be as part of a live Zoom event, or a prerecorded presentation, it may feature readings from a socially distanced venue (or not, depending on the situation). More details will hopefully clarify this soon.

Overcoming isolation was part of our original Freiraum concept and perhaps it would be interesting to see if or how our experience in recent months has changed or developed our view on the subject?

We'd also be keen to celebrate our creativity through poetry, spoken word, music, art, film, and how we live our lives in our own free space.

If you'd like to take part, have any questions about the event, or want to arrange any prerecorded material please let me know. I know 31st October isn't that far away but nothing focuses the mind like a deadline!

Philip Hewitson, poet wrangler – 14th September 2020

Link to 'SpeakEasy meets Freiraum' on YouTube

John Charlesworth

A FEW PERSONAL REFLECTIONS ON A VARIETY OF DIFFICULTIES EXPERIENCED IN THE FUNCTIONING OF ARTISTIC ACTIVITIES IN A WIDER CONTEXT OF PRIVATION IN THE CORONAVIRUS PANDEMIC.

For many the changed atmosphere, tighter conditions and opportunities for reaching an audience and for connecting with fellow practitioners have given rise to loud complaint and special pleading. Some, by all accounts, are giving up, but perhaps more are becoming more resourceful, digging deeper. There have been inventive solutions and compromises, usually deploying digital technology in specific and complex ways. I watched the abbreviated, audience-free version of The Proms, and enjoyed it immensely. Having said that, this level of performance is really of a different order in terms of funding, support and professional competence to stand as a template for more grassroots productions. Except as a demonstration of upping your game when unusual pressure is applied. It is conceivable that the anxiety of insecurity incentivises as well as the opposite.

At a more popular level sport, itself embodying, of course, much art and drama but applied crucially to a competitive essence, has been necessarily cast in an altered light. Playing to the gallery has been more or less stripped out and events have taken on the aspect of a determined exercise, determined, that is to exclude the sense of its unreality. By adherence, no doubt, to hard business practices, as well as a variety of big and small conjuring tricks so far the "elite" elements are managing to stay afloat or at least in existence.

Earlier in the new dispensation there was the added entertainment for the t.v. viewer of football matches of recorded crowd noises quite unrelated of course to actual passages of play and giving the impression of a game played in front of a crowd of idiots or drunks.

More germane to my own work, an online painting exhibition to replace a physical one (in Edinburgh) represented in effect no more and no less than the usual substitute fare, swallowed up as it is

in a great amorphous mass of digital imagery. No genuine sense of scale, texture, depth, technique. I personally, were I a purchaser of art, would never commit to buying a painting on the strength of a leisurely perusal of a little screen, and with this online show of my own work I never remotely felt the likelihood of sales, which indeed there weren't, or of any chance of palpable interaction whatever.

On Songs of Praise, in a programme devoted to The Pilgrim Fathers, I saw a performance by Seth Lakeman in an empty room somewhere in Plymouth and playing and singing with such authentic feeling and exuberance as to transcend the seemingly unhelpful context. A man in no way separated from his muse.

I heard recently on Radio 2 Jo Whiley's erstwhile "Infatuation", a new Radiohead song. Thom Yorke in a Leonard Cohen-like monotone and to a hypnotic backing articulating, I imagine, his introspective take on present circumstances. It was clearly not aimed at the likes

of me but I wasn't immune to its power of attraction, a mostly predictable mix of self-indulgent faux-gloom just shy of genuine gloom but managing to clear an adolescent miasma of indeterminate values of light and shade. There are realities you grow out of and ones you grow into.

We were lucky enough to have our daughter and granddaughters from Wales to stay just before things tightened up again. I never direct their attention towards my paintings, of which the house is full. However I've been doing a lot of new ones and to my surprise and delight I noticed the younger girl, 8, starting to show a furtive interest in them. She does happen to be child very much with her own ways, in fact a bit eccentric like me, and what strikes me is — and this has a wider application and also shines like a light in the present murk — that she finds herself able to see paintings without the prior intrusion of needing an explanation as a way in. Let art speak to you, if it will, let it present itself to its best advantage.

If it has joy within it, free that joy with an affectionate eye.

    In conclusion I am frankly of the opinion that the price exacted by isolation at this time is heavier for individuals, especially the old and especially those with few resources — mental, physical, material. Such people aren't difficult to imagine and empathise with, their loss and loneliness and sadness cannot really be compared with the frustrations, fears and lost opportunities of otherwise hale, if maybe not hearty, artists. The plight of the latter is real, and it impinges on my own experience as a self-employed painter, but it engenders sympathy rather than compassion. Art needs a heart to justify its considerable existential privilege, and it should imaginatively dare to go where privilege has never set foot.

The Gift

Josephine Dickinson

The birds fall silent.
Enki rests his dark head.
Pestilence comes,
vastness, destruction.

In the wastes
shepherds carry on.
Words shine
but hearts are empty.

In spring she left
the underground waters,
her attendants in front and behind,
with sceptre and mace,
fenced round by the demons.

He is absent,
the young poet,
as cities are emptied,
stripped of his power.

Namma, mother of the gods,
carries their tears
to him as he sleeps.

'My son, wake up!
How can you sleep
as creatures suffer?

Take your gift.
Make new gods
out of the soil.'

Not Flocking, Following
(22 March 2020)
Janette Ostle

As the world panicked
and flocked
to places, same places;
ignoring warnings
they thought others would follow
so why should they follow,
they followed
to places, same places.

As the world disregarded
and flocked
I walked to a place, a usual place
'round the block
where life was found blooming
in bloom from a crack,
a crack
in a crumbling wall.

Where the world followed
not flocked
earth was found clearing,
clearing in waters
with clearing blue sky
as the sun pulled my cheek
I felt hope
for a world
that man, kind
will now follow.

When Time Stopped (The Richardson Street Blues)
S. J. C. Hymers

The streets are empty
The roads are silent.
No birdsong can be heard.
No planes to be seen in the sky.

No children out playing.
No breeze can be felt.
No dogs barking!
No sign of human life.

It's almost like time has stopped!
It's like the hands of a clock have stopped.
It's like time has stopped flowing.
It's like time has gone out of sync!

Shops are still
Doors kept shut.
Windows kept closed.
Families kept alone.

Will time ever flow again?
Will any noise be heard again?
Will life ever return to normal?
Will things ever be the same again?

Only time will tell as the saying goes.
Only time will heal old wounds, hopefully!
Time and tides will flow again!
When the stars burn bright in the sky.
When time stopped!
Oh! I've got the Richardson Street Blues!!

Conversation with my father
Kelly Davis

You once told me about a show you'd seen.
A troupe of deaf-blind actors made bread on stage,
sitting at a long table, with bowls of flour,
adding water, sugar, salt, yeast,
mixing, kneading,
telling their stories
while the bread baked,
then offering the loaves
to those who watched.

And as you spoke,
tears filled your eyes, and mine,
until you could no longer speak.
We thought of those actors
in their dark, silent world,
feeding the audience
with something more than bread.
And we wept for the silence between us,
for the words never said.

Note: The show mentioned in this poem is called *Not by Bread Alone*. It was developed and directed by Adina Tal, at the Nalaga'at Center, Tel Aviv.

This poem was selected for Luke Jerram's Bread Poetry project: https://www.lukejerram.com/breadpoetry/

Trapped inside the tower
Lou Rodger

Once upon a while ago
I was trapped in my mind, no room to grow

My mind it chose to build a wall
I built it wide, and built it tall

It became a tower, dark inside
A haven, safe for me to hide

The windows were kept barred and locked
To keep out those who laughed and mocked

I thought I'd be missed, I must've been wrong
Nobody seemed to notice I'd gone

And when they came near, I thought they would gloat
So I pushed them away and they drowned in the moat

It didn't take long for them to stop trying
And nobody saw I was quietly dying

So I filled the walls with stacks of books
And cosy little reading nooks

And I lived through other people's tales
Though I never left my mental jail

But one day I found it hard to breathe
Began to daydream of how to leave

But the walls began to close on me
Whenever I dreamt of being free

So I tried to escape but the walls were too tough
All of my strength and it wasn't enough

I didn't know why but I thought I was strong
Maybe I had just been stuck for too long

I tried to dig down but the ground was too thick
My wrists were bleeding from beating the bricks

I'd all but chosen just to give in
My resolve and strength worn far too thin

But as I lay there broken and sore
I realised I'd never locked the door

Without You There's Nothing To Do
Harry Cartwright-Smith

Sometimes life is such a nasty place
You live, you eat, you work till you're beat
and there's sweat running down your face
Your manmade structures don't all look the best
SHUT YA GOB, DO THE JOB, YOU DON'T NEED A REST!
But think of all the good things that are here, and worth you living
You don't see any stars when you're buried and in heaven
Sometimes there's things in life
Where I've never got a clue
And then there's the things I like to share with you,
Ye-eh!
Cos without you there's nothing to do
Ye-eh
Cos without you there's nothing to do

Life gets the better of us all
Climb a happy mountain, or see a fountain
either way, you're gonna fall
Don't expect a day to be your day!
Hope was at the bottom of the box anyway
But you don't need to go jump off a roof
Hope is out there somewhere, go outside and see the proof.
You may be suffering due to life
But hey, I suffer too.
And I'm happy to spend my time with you
Ye-eh
Cos without you there's nothing to do
Ye-eh
Cos without you there's nothing to do

Life is a business meeting in which you have to sit
It's a quite-hard videogame that you can't rage-quit
Find the secret mini-games, enjoy them while they last
And learn a bit about the past.
So think about what you wanna do, think a little more,
You don't get a second chance if you're dead on the floor.
People question why we're alive, they haven't got a clue
But my reason for survival is YOU!
Ye-eh
Cos without you there's nothing to do
Ye-eh!
Cos without you there's nothing to do!

This is not a poem about the coronavirus
Clare Louise Roberts

This is not a poem about the coronavirus.
So don't worry you don't have to leave
Although could you still stay 6 feet away from me, please?

No this is not a poem about the topic we all know
We're all thinking about it anyway
And I know a lot of us have been affected by it

Creatively speaking.

It's all we write about
And every piece of new writing
At next year's Fringe festival
Is going to be
Set in a lockdown!
Or about something contagious
Or a global pandemic
Or a cute and quirky little look
At the everyday people and families and lives who

Were tragically affected.

No,
I'm not going to bore you with the same material
And more importantly than boring an audience
(I said what I said)
I'm going to show some respect
To those who unlike me are
Really having to deal with it

Therefore I declare
That this is not a poem about the coronavirus.
So
don't
panic.

I will not delve into wordplay with
The face masks we wear
To protect ourselves physically
As well as emotionally.

Dedicating prose to the NHS
And all of the key workers
Would be a very sweet idea
But that would be highlighting
What I do not wish to highlight.

Because this is not a poem
About the topic we all know
It's not about lamenting over Covid-19
And pondering our new concept
Of time and normal
It's not about what-ifs and if only we had different leaders
And all of our Mayors were Italian
And our prime minister was
That cool lady from New Zealand.

No.

This poem
This poem

This poem

Unfortunately, like me, is going nowhere right now
Because we're all stuck
In isolated lockdown
And everything's sad
And I've got all the time in the world

And I'm spending it
Trying not to think
Not to worry
About...

The thing I keep telling you I'm not going to talk about.

So I guess the person who is creatively stifled is me.
The one who is thinking about it anyway
But somehow not yet bored

The one who does wish that we had better leaders
And that people would admit they wore masks
More often than you can see them

I'm the one who is fearful of talking about it
In an art form
Because I want to be respectful
And not make art
Which is the wrong kind of painful

And I'm dreading all of the future
Work we're going to see
That will be an insensitive exploit
Of what's currently
Going on.
I just don't trust us enough to not get it wrong.

So I'm not going to do anything of the sort
For now

I'm still creating
As well as
Still worrying

There are plenty of things to say
But I don't have to talk about Covid-19

Unless I'm confident in my delivery
And confident in my message
Which I'm clearly
Not right now.

Because people are scared, they're hopeful, crying, dancing
This isn't picking sides
This is one person in the isolated
Space of an hour
And I understand
That as an artist I yield power
So –

This is not a poem about the coronavirus.

But if it was

Would what I say
Be respectful
And loving enough?

Let's Hew
James Scott Riddick

let's hew some shapes
out of this soft text rock
maybe place it in a mortar
work it till it's a fine powder
sow it over some furrows
scatter over onions as they caramelise
or insufflate and see what it does to our minds

the first cut is the worst cut
infinitely bigger than any cut before
it makes your heart feel
too big for its cage
and a stable grip a memory
or a myth or a memory of a myth
I have never cut an umbilical cord
so I won't compare the two
but I couldn't help the association in my mind
and admitting that seems the right thing to do
or worthwhile procrastination
from what is actually the right thing to do

that being whatever doesn't hurt
someone else
throwing the biggest rock you can heft
into an empty lake
kicking discarded cardboard
like you've wanted to kick people before
telling yourself you want to die
but only in your own head
all which you can harness
when you bring your implement
into contact with the rawwordmatterblock
each a different screwdriver head
with its own impression
irreversibility as common ground
all you can do is start

Umwelt[*]
Fernando Smith

Like radiation, we cannot yet see hope.
If we feel it, then we do so
only in the way water is sensed,
passing across our bodies as
we swim the Channel.

I have imagined a machine that
looks into dark rooms.
It translates that part of the world
otherwise invisible, even
to well-practised eyes.
Until its production-lines open,
we will watch for movement
in the bushes around our perimeter.

Let us now be like the passing of the seasons.
The leaving and returning of swallows.
The lost star reappearing in the constellation
of a new union.

[*]Umwelt - the world as it is experienced by a particular organism

A JOURNEY WITH NO PLAN, NO IDEA...

One Step at a Time
Valerie Moody

Breathe
This is the world
Take your place in it
One step at a time

Time
To end this retreat
This self-isolation
You impose on yourself

Disguise
The fear that you feel
The panic inside
Put a smile on your face

Talk
To the girl in the shop
Just say hello
Then thank you, goodbye

Relax
Hold your head high
No-one will know
How hard you find this

Success!
The first steps are taken
To rejoin society
To overcome this isolation

Everywhere

John Chambers

This river, this wind
This enchantment, this culture
This summer, this idyll
This madness, this emotion
This religion, this friendship
This belonging, this headfuck
This comedy, this anomaly
This child, this family
This nirvana, this house
This amazement, this stranger
This adrenaline, this poem,
This dome, this curiosity
This kiss, this solution
This sex, this bliss.

This dream, this touch, this joy, this room
Is everywhere
This hope, this garden, this street, this life
Is everywhere.

This picture, this news
This story, this bus
This journey, this cruelty
This Eden, this sun
This daughter, this mother
This gun, this father
This bomb, this car
This word, this plant
This boundary, this grave
This rain, this endless rain
This road, this mask
This book, this back
This lake, this walk
This hammer, this nail
This fucking Daily Mail
This shirt, this scent
This hate, this division
This trope, this meme

This hat, this food
This smell, this rock
This fire, this morning
This leap, this plane
This passion, this drug
This wall, this wire
This dance, this memory
This war, this dust
This night, this sky

This look, this friend, this time, this world
Is everywhere
This moment, this desire, this feeling, this love
Is everywhere.

Photograph
Craig Davidson

Lockdown poem
Peter Robinson

Reality isn't what it used to be,
Lockdown life isn't how it's meant to be,
Life isn't free it has responsibility,
Not just to yourself but also to me,
Social distancing isn't just imaginary,
Youngsters now ignoring coronavirus risks incessantly,
Please remember in your rush back to normality,
Do it right, protect yourself and please don't kill me!!

Photograph
Craig Davidson

Lockdown
Marc Robinson

Coming out of lockdown
Marc Robinson

Easter Sunday Morning, Wigton
(12 April 2020)
Janette Ostle

As blossom laid abed, abed on winter's leaves
unwoken by the church bells, once carried on the breeze
Belted Will watched over the silence from his walls
dandelions roared from the cracks as resilient ivy falls

over empty bridges, over empty roads, where
tulips wait by empty tracks, train-spotting with due care.
Decorative tree twigs where painted eggs are posed
sit beneath a hand-writ note on a window stating 'closed';

closed until further notice, signed off, with a 'thank you'
below a 'thank you NHS', all forever in your lieu.
Framed quotation in a window, 'good friends are like a star';
these times where we can't see them, show exactly where they are.

Belisha beacon blinked and winked, it's safe now to proceed
across his empty crossing, essential worker, his good deed.
Floral adorned fountain, our well loved centrepiece
instructs four acts of mercy and, hopes mercy will increase.

A distanced bird flies over the silence of the street
back to nest of safety, she'll wait for throstle fleet.
'My heart leaps up when I behold a rainbow in the sky'
words closed inside the library, words unreturned still fly.

Tissue papered gratitude so rightly recognise
hard, hard working workers; who were once unrecognised.
Empty church, unopened on the day it's usually packed;
closed first time in a lifetime to keep its flock intact.

Finery's not needed, comfort clothes prevail
as we grow grey together, true colours will unveil.
Above Memorial Garden, flag reminds us of a past
a past that's been endured; with washed hands, we can last.

School drive signs 'no entry', no longer just one way.
An abrupt end of era, our future's next essay.
Trees of learning tower a daffodil avenue
they all avoid my shadow, one metre timesed by two.

Pharmacy and Doctors, briefly sleep, a well-earned rest
queue markers still await them, tomorrow brings next test.
Petrol pumps, like sentries, by empty garage floor
clock my hour's exercise to place chocolate by Mam's door.

I walk home feeling grateful; still shit down Dog Shit Alley
still smoke, from factory smoke, as Mary-Anne's still rally
with gadgies by our Pump and Lamp, they've stood by worse before;
still stand, still hope, still waiting for a clearer life once more.

"Whoever lays his hand on me to govern me is a usurper and tyrant, and I declare him my enemy."
– Pierre-Joseph Proudhon

Catalan Cowls
Fernando Smith

From Catalan cowls to Manchester
cobbles, always here
this tender arm
this rock of shoulder
this open heart
this absolute light.

These people, they endured
the gravest storms.
Bit their lips and cracked a joke.

No more.

Across the way, a field lies
waiting to be reclaimed.
A seed in soil watered with
four hags' portents.

You think the oak will submit
to breath so foul, spat out
from lungs corroded with
deceits and vanities?

No more.

No more.

Elsewhere... Something Happens
James Scott Riddick

the luxury to only worry
bursts in the mouth
not toxic
but it tastes
drained abscess
lingering like

garlic on the breath
aggressive inconvenience
in the face of an indifferent date
go home
deflated, but not forever

when the water is high again
you're OK, plenty of time
to get out the way
a little float left in you
if things get closer

back out again
average day
as far as the eye can see

elsewhere, you couldn't pin it on a map
something happens
the details buried too deep
in a guardian article

without realising
you search for incentive
come back empty-handed

'Self Portrait'

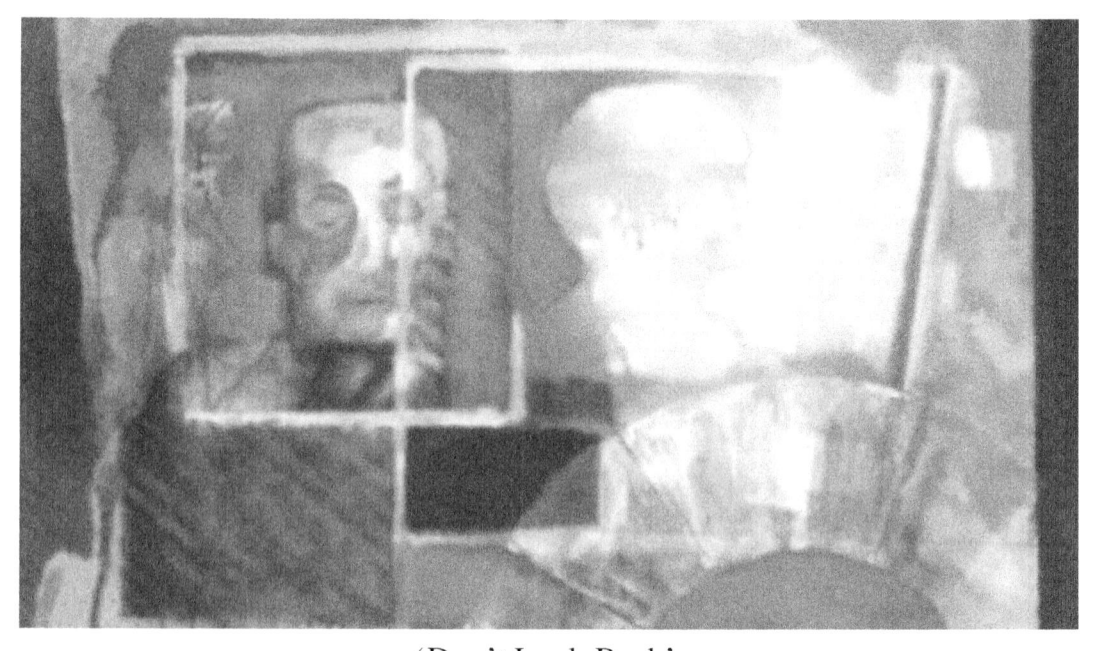

'Don't Look Back'

Artwork
Kevin O'Connor

'Cloud'

'Solway Sun'

Borderlines
Ally Barr

Borders are transitory, in-between, on the limit kinds of places
Dispute, death, walls, fences, searches
Concrete outposts, barbed wire, flags, uniforms, passports,
inclusion, exclusion, discrimination,
arbitrary lines traverse oceans, landscapes, paper, politics, minds

Here in Cumbria I inhabit both sides of the border
North and South, for and against, here and there,
2020 and whatever the future holds

Not that the eternal moon breath tide would know
as it ebbs and flows, pulls and drags out
across the muddy Solway

I once tried to walk across the sand flats
out to the border line
But it kept shifting and jumping from coast to coast

The cloud filled mirror illusion collapsed
My feet started sinking and in the end I didn't really know where I stood

Photograph
Craig Davidson

Together Apart
Valerie Moody

I'm all alone
In my living room
About to chat
To my kids on Zoom

My lovely boy
My gorgeous girl,
It's lonely here
In lockdown world

We can talk
But cannot touch
I miss them both
So very much

And if we meet
We cannot hug
In case we catch
The Covid bug

Then as we talk
Across the miles
My grandson's face
Pops up and smiles

At Christmas he
Was still quite small
Now he seems
So very tall

I used to visit
We used to play
Now I'm not
Allowed to stay

I speak to him
Whenever I can
So he won't
Forget his Gran

Cos most of all
It's him I miss;
We say 'Goodbye'
He blows a kiss

'Love you Gran
See you soon!'
And with a wave
They're gone from Zoom

Once again
I'm on my own
In lockdown world
And all alone

*Whilst we keep apart
colour arches together
a rainbow of hope*

Janette

And we painted rainbows
Philip Hewitson

Life put on hold
A danger to the young and the old
We came together as a nation
Each week a celebration
Of NHS, carers, essential workers whose stories are so often untold

And there's a rainbow in my heart
Cos I'm happy we can play our part
But I'm sad cos times are bad
For so many in the arts

Who is there to sing a song
Who will right us when we're wrong
Actors telling stories for the screen or on the stage
Scriptwriters and the poets are the strolling players of our age

Where's the orchestra?
Where's the dancer at the ballet?
Where's the stage show?
Where's the singer with the band?
Where's the clown telling jokes?
Where's the painter supposed to show their pictures?
Where's the new film on at the flicks?

But when will it end, and where is the help?
Is there a long term or easy, quick fix?
The truth is nobody knows
So we paint rainbows and hope
We paint the rainbows
We paint the rainbows

INTERCONTINENTAL TEA

Ally Barr

She was stripped of all character,
concealed in a cupboard
for three generations.
One day, out of the blue,
my mother acknowledged her.

My ancestor, Alicia Wiltshire,
parents 'native', unnamed.
Married to Alexander Stewart
on 22nd of September, eighteen fifty,
in Saugar, Central India.

She looks out of the window
of four, Horse Market Close,
wonders what the future holds
for her Anglo Madras family.

Here in this grey border town,
not a monkey or temple in sight.
No colourful saris or floury chapattis.
Cold drizzle blurs the window pane.
Distant almond eyes gaze
across oceans and centuries.

She turns and pours herself a cup of tea,
a welcome link between continents.
Prays to Durga that truth
and justice will reign.

One hundred and fifty years later
I look in the mirror;
see a merging of faces,
feel the heat of an Indian sun
rising over Cumbria.

Photograph
Craig Davidson

I ate the whole cake
David Simmons

A sudden slice of governance: the ingredients are social legalities, biting rules of personal interaction, that make us gulp. No mixing of households, no licking spatulas with friends. Everyday recipes too salty by far to swallow.

My lodger hesitates, as if deciding whether to open the front door with sticky fingers. Then passes over the food of comfort for emotional needs, and reluctantly leaves.

My home now has the air, the texture, of an over-baked cake. The end of a lifetime's sharing feels like heartburn. I'm not injured or ill, but I think my mind is bleeding.

I quietly seek to fill the void and decamp to the brick-walled garden, hoping sun and fresher air will heal the wound.

From the house I take some familiar items with me: a pair of ducks have seen better days, two cats sit reading, various survivors of the Ark, all equally deserving.

I think they'll ease the dialogue with the flowers, birds and bees. I record images to retain some humour, a form of artistic exercise, and collect delphinium seeds.

As the hours, days and weeks turn into months, I sense the bleeding cease.

I start each summer's day with a dab of cold water, careful not to disturb the delicate scar.

My last lodger and me, we have a common food compulsion, a nose for the discounts, and we share on social media our small achievements, maintaining our differing tastes, trying new food combinations, and that for us has the consistency of closure.

Weeping willow wept
light entered every droplet
reflecting rainbows

Janette

Poem as a Role Handover
James Scott Riddick

poem as a role handover
I hope this finds you well
It's important to remember
no matter how counterintuitive it may feel
to always...
except when you absolutely shouldn't
really the position is as much me
as it was mine
you'll have to untangle
the matter that's left
the strands that grew
to fit around me

58

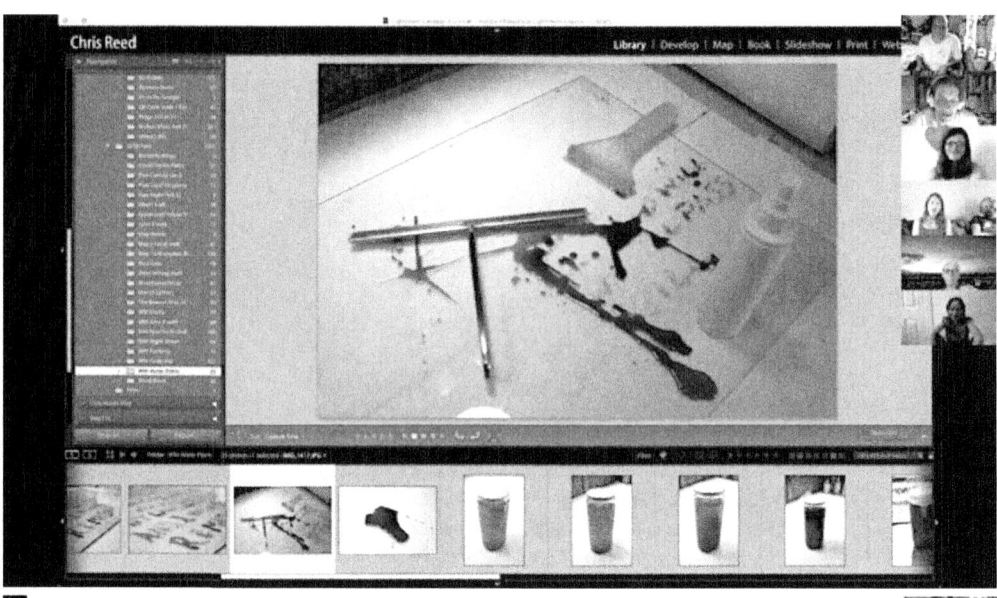

Walton Moss
Chris Reed

You are growing but unchanged
You are tracked but trackless
You are drab but bejewelled
You are prairie and summit
You are old but still young
You are open but closed
You are empty but full
You are lake and hill
You are dry but wet
You have outlived us all
You will outlive us all
My shadow will pass and I will be gone
You will remain

Chris shares the result of his experimental poem made from the juice of blackberries mixed with sugar, essentially blackberry jam. Susan declares 'It's a poetry jam!'

24th June 2020, SpeakEasy – online.

TERRITORY
Ally Barr

Lichened rocks, weathered,
bog-bleached, catch light.
Long finger bone protrusions
beckon from black peat.

Blackcaps, stonechats,
skylarks, wagtails, ring ouzels,
flit, chatter, weave, soar,
scold, watch, bob, squabble.

Stray feathers catch in sedges.
Telltale pellets, silver-furred,
hold remnants of bone,
tiny skulls, grass-cupped.

White spatters cairns
and boundary markers.
Slow weathering ghosts
claimed by birds.

Artwork
Craig Davidson

The Tragedy of the Peacock Prince
Ros Edwards

Fabulous, exotic creature
Turning the heads of all who see you
With your shock of electric blue
Studded with emerald eyes
You raise your tail feathers high
And shimmer.
You know you are magnificent
A prince among the garden birds
The stranger in this landscape.
You watch the cock pheasant call
And see his hens come running.
How you hate the pheasants
You chase them from the food
You are keeping it for your mate.
Each spring you are filled with hope
Standing tall you call loudly
Eyes scanning the horizon
Gazing longingly across the field
Day after day he calls
He is man in his prime
Handsome in his finery
But your display will never be seen
You are the only one of your kind
There are no peahens here
Your princess will not come
You are destined to be lonely
Most unhappy peacock
I see you hanging around the back door
Skulking now your finery has gone
Brown and white, ripples your wings
That hide the seeds of new growth
That will come to fruition next summer
When again you will strut your stuff, in vain
Alone, isolated and splendid
You are a tragic figure
A prince who will not fulfil his destiny

But imagine;
If you abandoned your roost
Left this citadel and went on a quest
To find that beautiful princess
And rescue her from the tower.
Because somewhere there is an aviary
Where an unhappy peahen
Afraid to go out in the world
Is waiting for her prince to come.
How unbearably sad
Are the broken dreams
Of lonely people who never meet.

Photograph
Ros Edwards

PARAKEETS IN THE PARK
Tony Hendry

Mary Anderson calling.
I'm right there, walking the dog,
in the park you're talking about.
Dashing ring-necked parakeets
in the trees by the playing fields,
as if this was Delhi or Lucknow.
I love the bonny green dazzlers.
Flash company for me.

Victoria Park in Glasgow!
Scotland's only breeding colony,
the most northerly parrot flock
on earth, screeching in my park,
barked at by my Jack Russell.
Joyous birds with coral beaks.
When I first set eyes on them,
it was magic. Pure glamourie.

The last man who phoned in
called my dears a marmite bird.
Me, I love marmite on my toast.
Another loon wanted them shot,
called them an invasive species.
No. They're versatile survivors
which find a place in nature.
Xenophobes are always with us.

The ants of Lisbon

Fernando Smith

The ants of Lisbon go about
their daily duties.
The ants of Lisbon care not for
the beauties of the garden.
The ants of Lisbon do not
appreciate Alfama squares
or stop to weep a Fado tear
a broken reverie
by the Tagus.
They go about their common task
without the knowledge
they will outlast
the likes of you and me
and all the art
there ever was
and ever there will be.
The ants of Lisbon
work and wait and do
not feign or hesitate
to contemplate their
winning role in history.

Poem from the future: The trees lead the way out of the gorge
Juliet Fossey

Year One; the locals planted
saplings. Little things wrapped
in rags from the women's washing.

Year Two; they watched half fail
and dust blow. Small towels coddled
the buds at night when the air was cool.

Year Three; the trees that live, have leaves.
Floods came, washed some away, but those
that stayed are stronger now and Jo counts them
each Sunday instead of going to church.

Year Four; disease has spread. The chimps of the gorge
have colds. A baby female has nearly died. Keeping them
alive is the only chance they have of joining forest outside.

Year Five; she has survived, not the biggest or strongest
but her genes must be good and there is hope of a new family.

Year Six; Timu, leader of 'Project Re-connect' has died. Everyone
is sad and he is buried in the gorge with his beloved chimps.

Year Seven; the trees are up to the children's knees, they've grown up
nurturing these saplings. Green flags now link the gorge with forest seven
kilometres away.

Year Eight; a butterfly ventures along this small corridor. Following a line, the route
any forager might take. From one leaf to the next, where she flies, others will follow.

Year Nine; baby chimps play at the edge of the gorge. Big eyes weigh the space
beyond. Curious genes will take the naughtiest or weakest or most excluded along the
line, the cover just necessary to venture out and thrive.

The moon poured light
through heavy curtains
a cloud draped a blanket
around Skiddaw's shoulder

Artwork
Janette Ostle

Spiral Down

Susan Cartwright-Smith

A biorhythmic pause
Is like a drumbeat, heartbeat,
Carrying news that time has stilled,
And craving hearts, not craven
Take up that beat, surround
And symphonise in sympathy.
Echoing quiet is encroached –
The yearning need for space's chasm
Is constantly denied.
I am the centre of the target,
Concentric circles closing in.
The shadow of another's body
Falls across the path of me
And presses close behind.
I strain to hear
The newly silenced birds,
And different blooms shake
Their heavily scented heads.
The circle turns, memories fade,
So I look up –
From the centre of this circle
I look up, blink,
In the strengthening rays,
And spiral out.

Towards Mockerkin

Craig Davidson

A clutch of bent oaks clings steadfastly atop a lonely Lakeland fell.

Time, their seasoned master - not just gnarly stubbornness.

Yearning for embraces from inquisitive kids,

Two at a time, trying and failing to touch fingertips

Around their vast, comforting trunks.

Eager to share their catkins and fill tiny acorn cups

With stories of innocence and secret melancholy.

Trees scarred by meteorological sorcery and hastily-etched love.

Down below the glistening slate and damp bracken,

Across the water and between the hedgerows beyond,

A derelict cottage stares back in quiet indignance -

Forlorn, for sale - forever it now seems.

Rustic, ramshackle remnants - persistent memories of a fragmented past.

Nearby, a black-faced ewe, detached from the other stragglers in the flock,

Stands aloof, bleating plaintively skyward,

As if to warn of others, here before, who have silently passed.

From here looking upwards, a couple of oaks - now seemingly entwined -

Were estranged on the last visit, two summers ago.

Joined now in supplication, they pray for local buyers

With young ones or a baby on the way.

Two years on, a distant, forgotten church creaks under the weight of Harvest offerings.

Children sprout up, bold as brassicas through leafy compost.

Tuneful carollers lighten the mood of a dark, deeply snowbound December.

Their voices fading as they make for the pub amidst an off-key snowball fight.

Then, under the wistful gaze of ghostly Celtic Kings,

Youngsters skim stones across Mockerkin Tarn in Spring,

And on a roughly rectangular foot-long slab of Lakeland slate:

'Gethsemane' - writ large in duck-egg blue with no two 'e's quite the same -

Adorns the entrance to a newly-renovated cottage.

"*They'd wanted 'Eden'-summat*" 'til the postman groaned he'd "*fow-wer aw-riddy*".

Between the Lines
Barbara Renel

High tide. The woman is taking photographs of the child flying a kite on the beach. The glare from the sun obscures the image. Maybe chance will catch the moment – blue skies, the kite tugging at the thread that binds it to the child, laughter filling the silence.

I'm flying, the child shouts – oyster catcher, lapwing, curlew.

Turning tide. The woman scrambles through brambles, gorse, climbs over worn masonry blocks to the pier end.

Where's the merry-go-round, the candy floss, the gold fish in a plastic bag, the slot machines, the tearoom? the child asks.

The woman ratches though rubble, broken bricks, picks up a – rivet? bolt? flange? She stands beside six cast iron stanchions, remnants of the viaduct that once linked north to south. In the shallow waters on the far side of the estuary, fishermen are haaf-netting. The child waves, but they don't see her.

Low tide. The woman crosses the saltmarsh and walks towards the Irish Sea. The estuary, an expansive, strange landscape of tidal sands, mudflats, silence. She searches, picks up shells – pink tellins, cockles.

If Scotland is over there and we live in England, where are we now? the child asks.

No man's land, she replies. Greyscale images of concrete walls, barbed wire, watch towers, news reports of deaths in that desolate space between east and west – another border.

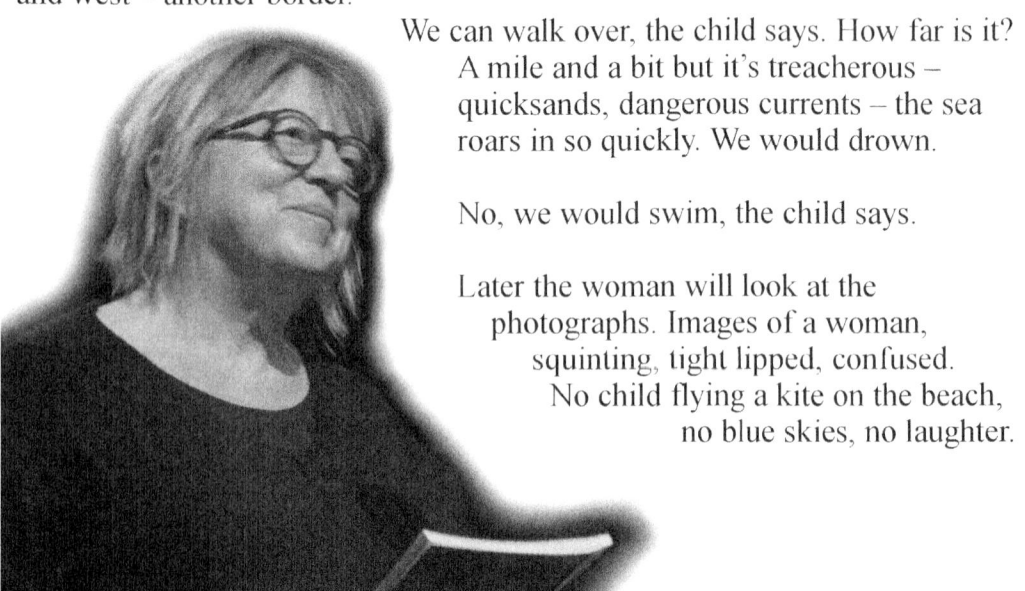

We can walk over, the child says. How far is it? A mile and a bit but it's treacherous – quicksands, dangerous currents – the sea roars in so quickly. We would drown.

No, we would swim, the child says.

Later the woman will look at the photographs. Images of a woman, squinting, tight lipped, confused. No child flying a kite on the beach, no blue skies, no laughter.

Resonance

Josephine Dickinson

The physics of bells is that of the virion.
Earth speaks through their voice
beyond the human.
'If a stone could speak,' said Galway, but it does speak.
Born of stars, returning to stars.
We are the wind blown in the trees,
the air of the waiting valley.
We trust, live in the resonance.
Living is more than knowing.

A vine stands, a metal vine,
clusters dangle above,
ready for picking.
The metal canes — ten —
stretch, tend, tender, tentative, attentive,
in the tent of Moses and of Abraham,
with the ten commandments,
their head in a metal cage,
their eight arms and two cordons,
arranged as a keyboard, a key.

What is inside, what is outside the window?
The room where she has control
        — so little! only ten notes (not even sure of the tuning) — the room,
womb, stanza where a note gestates,
a room from which the note will venture,
a journey with no plan, no idea.
Living is more than knowing.

Up and down the forty nine steps,
hard red hat on a chair blocking the top flight,
she catches a glimpse of movement.
A chair, a cupboard, an unlit fire.
The key in the door.
The wedge, the light switch.
Dark stairwell, two flights,
two doors, to a store,
then a room with a long low table,
two narrow windows ahead,

with cobwebbed diamond panes,
a latch door, a light switch
in the dark, the quiet, the cool, the dust,
funeral cards on a plinth.
Living is more than knowing.
Vulnerable, limited,
in the place of the Trinity,
a bird raises its feeble wings,
hesitates before taking the food.

The Angel marking time
since the Ice Age,
the one that reaches above and below
out of ten,
the Angelus bell,
Cross Fell enjoins to gladden hearts
with prosperity, wisdom, love,
beauty, well-being —
sadness as well.
The seasons sound,
the year, the perceptible,
the 2020 frequencies,
the lockdown,
the return to the Shepherd
who put them here
in the pristine meadow.

It started with friendship,
camaraderie, laughter in the spire,
dancing, singing in the street,
moss dancing,
no knowing what to play next,
the limits of agency,
in the dark,
not knowing where it goes,
how she will trip up.
We carry on, we trust,
live in the energy.
Living is more than knowing.

Photography
Craig Davidson

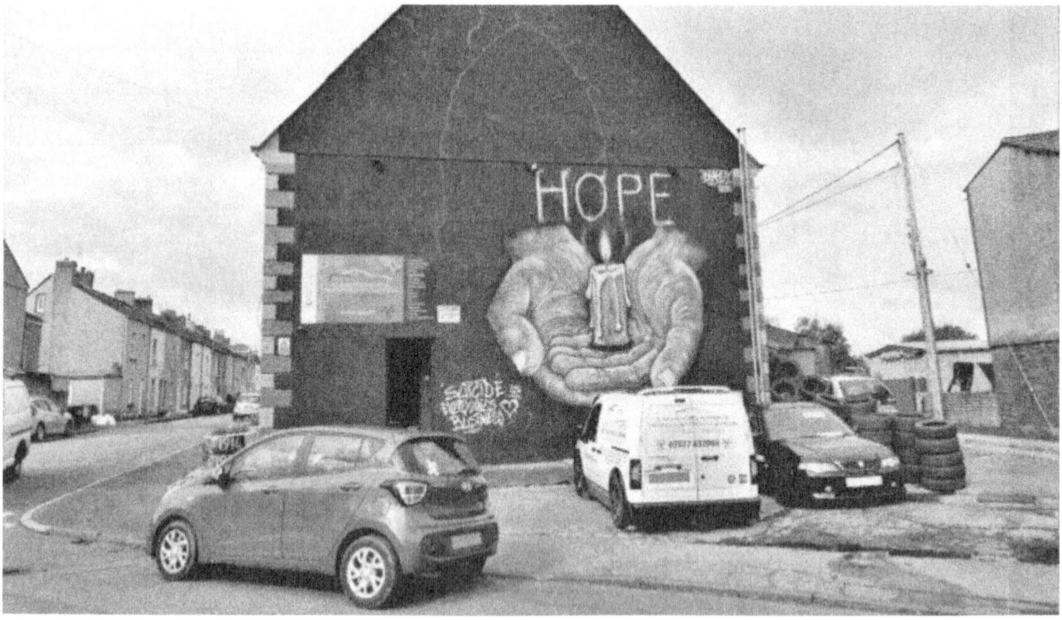
HOPE

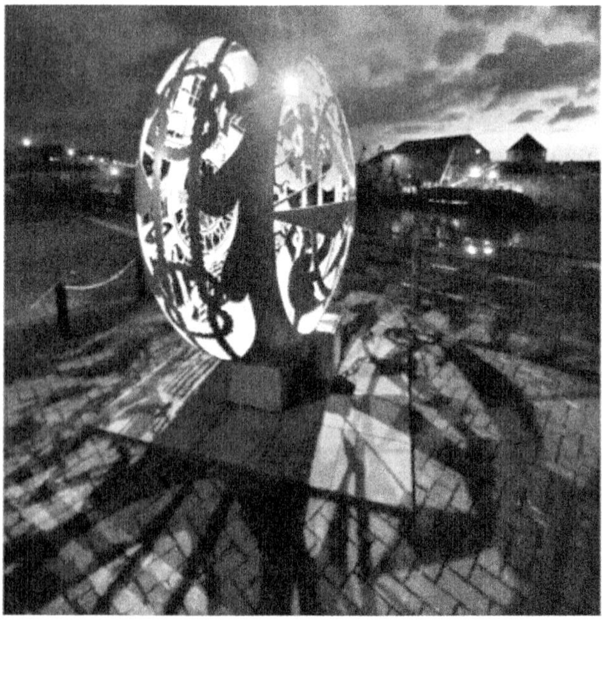

HOW FAR WILL HOPE STRETCH...

WE ARE CLAY
Ally Barr

Timeworn towers speak across millennia
from Cumbria to Mesopotamia.
Hands scooped clay by Solway reed beds
and dug between the Tigris and Euphrates.
The Tower of Babel searched high for God.
By now He may have regretted forming
the shape of man in the Garden of Eden.

At the Empire's edge, Hadrian's Wall
and the river Eden, *Itouna* of rushing water,
yielded to a silver sea expanse.
Craftsmen pressed stamps into wet tiles,
preserving legions, emperors, the Empire.
Waxen masks peeled from the dead
stared blankly from wall niches.

*Come let us make bricks and bake
them thoroughly.* King James Bible.
Shape, stack, dry, kiln, fire, build.
Clay mingles with cobalt and sand.
Classic colours; Cumbrian Red, Fletton,
Staffordshire Blues, Accrington Bloods,
Silver Oxfordshire, London Browns.

Crumbling, powdery, smoothed, flecked.
Crevices are crammed with particles;
root, mineral, animal, shell, fish, petals.
Carboniferous atoms interconnect.
Sediment crushed, weathered, layered.
Water gushes over mountains, eroding
feldspar, *mother of clay*.

Existence over, men are laid to rest
under a thin skin earth, equal with the clay.
Castles and churches, rise, fall, crumble.
Border lines and walls shift with dark tides;
Hadrian's, Berlin, Jericho, Troy. And more.
Walls designed by minds echo barriers within.

In The Whirlwind
James Ovens

In the whirlwind of repeated actions and conscious thoughts, the man of the modern age needs new light to breathe, to thrive and coexist. But of course some light isn't pure, isn't natural, a mirror in disguise. The earthy ground is scattered with dampened memories and the air spells a clouded thicket of poisonous perfumes. With the aid of a powerful friend the man weaves away from his cave of a stoned-in past. Though carved, rusted and bloody, the scent of new things combs to a ripple that leads to a hand. Words of silence transpire, the old diminishes and speckles bisect into something more dynamic. Human contact.

Me
Ally Barr

I am not white
I am freckled and a pinkish brown sort of colour
Sometimes tanned when the sun shines
I am not British, I am Scottish
And my genes tell a complicated story
that maps from Syria and India across Europe
I do not live in the United Kingdom
It is not united
I do not live in Great Britain
There's nothing great about it
And if I wear a t-shirt, what would the label say?
Me
Made in Scotland
Made on planet Earth
Handle with care

THE MAGIC OF WORDS
Ben Naga

NOW and HERE
Is the one and only
NOWHERE
Everywhere

One blink of the I
And back-to-front
NOW is reversed
For it is time

Time to be WON
The time has arrived
As NOW reveals
Its eternal nature

Pure consciousness
Unsullied
TIME is reversed
For it is EMIT

Time to emit
Heaven's light
As within, as without
Time to shine on

Heads bowed
Hands together
It is TIME NOW
Let us play

Baby's Best Heels
Fernando Smith

We gathered your shoes here
by the rubble
polished them bright
ready for a time
when you would return and
walk with us again.

A New Light
Valerie Moody

The light of my life has died
The world seems very dark outside
For hours and hours, I've cried
And in painful shadows I hide

I'm falling down a black hole
The darkness penetrating my soul
Bereavement has taken its toll
I don't seem to have any goal

Can I find one little spark
To burn a small hole in this dark?
I jump out of bed with the lark
And make my way up to the park

The day dawns clear and bright
My heart fills with hope at the sight
New day, new life, a new light

Perhaps I will be alright 😊

How Far Will Hope Stretch
James Scott Riddick

how far will hope stretch
before holes form
in its white face
a cartoon ghost
staring, blankly, back

a miniature person
maybe me, maybe you
runs over the top
a race against
hope's waning
structural integrity

no match for its sagging,
their tiny heft
only aiding gravity's
deconstruction

and the inevitable
happens, the ghost mouth
forms and expands
too fast
the person slides in

or do they dive
relishing
the opportunity
to join the dead

Second Wave
Kevin O'Connor

On a darkened stage
Pleading for normality
A second wave
Crashing on the shore
Promises that wash
Through sand
Untroubled beach
As if it were no more

Curtains closed
Hushed voices just a memory
Lighting- Exit- only
Silence; anticipation
Rehearsal of oblivion
Is this the way
Is this the way
Pandemic; Pandemonium

The Centre of the World Where We Will Meet
Fernando Smith

I'm touching you now
your neck, your head
stroking shoulders that hunch
and tense
in a room too dark for these aging eyes.
In a room where I recognise your
toolbox smell.
In a room where I was locked twenty-one years ago.

Your young body set on a
course of realising itself; learning
strength, application,
practising the swing of the hammer
shaving a flake from the lintel
crafting a finger of doweling into a segue
between locations.

And not even that

I'm holding you now
in this darkened room, with its black stars
where we pretend there isn't glass between us
where the air is not oil
nor our touch slithering from
a cheek without
sensing the cheek
remembering the cheek
recovering a muscle memory
like two old dancers recalling ancient steps
or articulating a fury with a loaded gesture.

And not even that

The time before the mist; we sat side by side
on the sofa listening to the cat's tongue licking milk
in the next room with its belly extended
like a loaf of bread.

It had forgotten how to stop feeding
and we no longer cared, now that
our veins had dried up with exhaustion
in the never-ending drought.

And not even that

Our words drowned in the digital stream
as we repeat the same news, attaching
great significance to our reporting.
We approach the Eucharist
We are serious as suicide.
As helpless as kites tugging the wind.
We have become the taut line suspended
between earth and sky.

And not even that

"Stay safe" we say
tears jamming our view out the window
where the tree is patient and even now
tenderly teasing a leaf from a scroll of bud.

"Stay safe" we say
choking on eight letters, two words
a sort of prayer, a dread, a portent,
maybe a lucky break.

And not even that

Instead this.

The distance between things made flesh and crammed
with a sour dreaming
that bothers our nights
that inflames our days
like a bruise changing colour.

"Stay safe" we say.

Indeed, stay safe
and come back to the centre of love
when the dirty air is still.

April 20th 2020

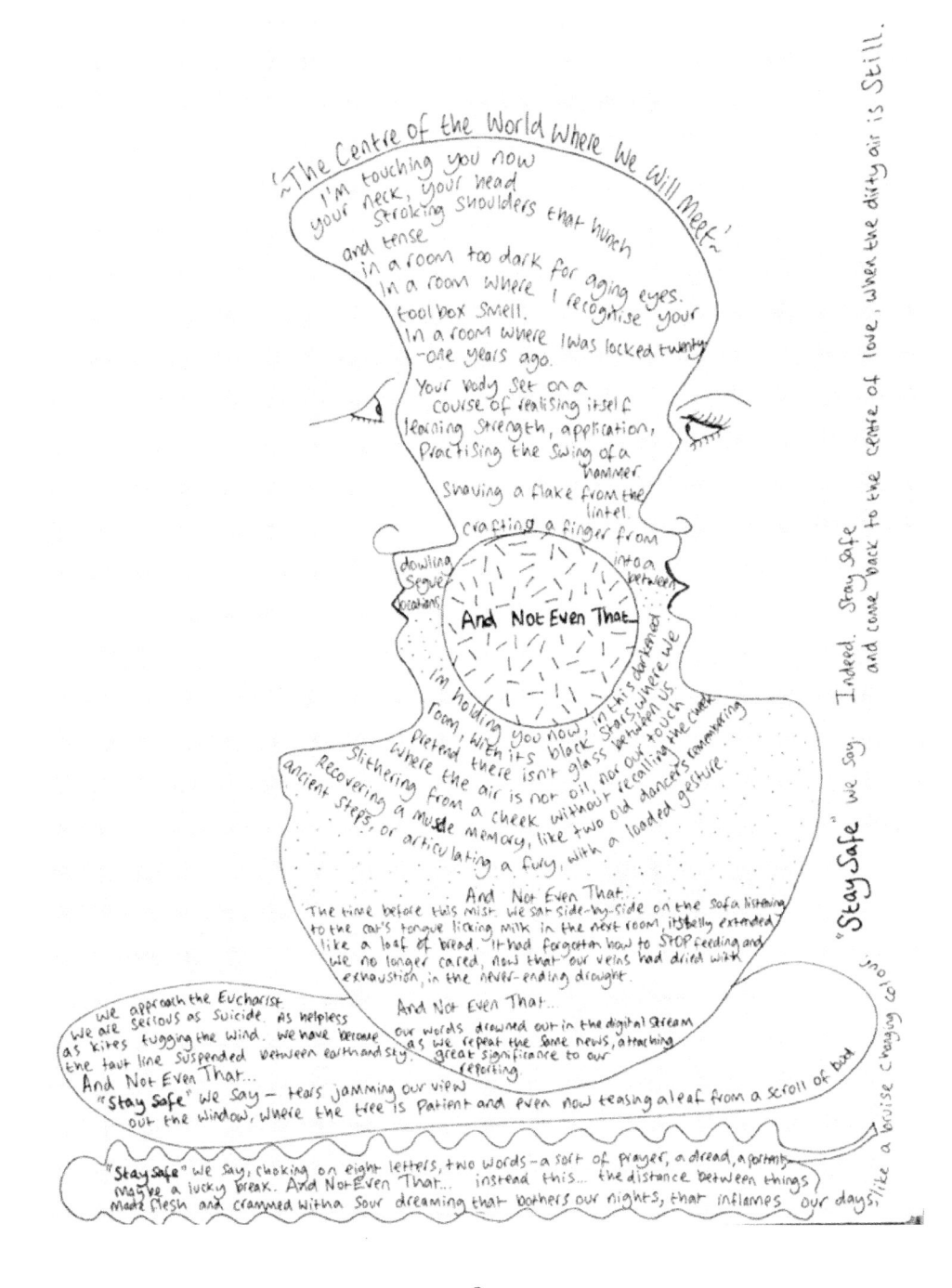

"The Centre of the World Where We Will Meet."

I'm touching you now, your neck, your head, stroking shoulders that hunch and tense in a room too dark for aging eyes. In a room where I recognise your toolbox smell. In a room where I was locked twenty-one years ago.

Your body set on a course of realising itself, learning strength, application, practising the swing of a hammer. Shaving a flake from the lintel. Crafting a finger from dowling. Sequel between notations.

And Not Even That...

I'm holding you now, in this darkened room, with its black stars where we pretend there isn't glass between us, where the air is not oil, nor our touch slithering from a cheek without recalling the cut. Recovering a muscle memory, like two old dancers remembering ancient steps, or articulating a fury, with a loaded gesture.

And Not Even That... The time before this mist, we sat side-by-side on the sofa listening to the cat's tongue licking milk in the next room, its belly extended like a loaf of bread. It had forgotten how to STOP feeding and we no longer cared, now that our veins had dried with exhaustion, in the never-ending drought.

And Not Even That... Our words drowned out in the digital stream as we repeat the same news, attaching great significance to our reporting.

We approach the Eucharist. We are serious as suicide, as helpless as kites tugging the wind. We have become the taut line suspended between earth and sky.

And Not Even That...

"Stay Safe" we say — tears jamming our view out the window, where the tree is patient and even now teasing a leaf from a scroll of bud.

"Stay safe" we say, choking on eight letters, two words — a sort of prayer, a dread, a portent, maybe a lucky break. And Not Even That... instead this... the distance between things made flesh and crammed with a sour dreaming that bothers our nights, that inflames our days like a bruise changing colour.

"Stay safe" we say. Indeed, stay safe and come back to the centre of love, when the dirty air is still.

Drifter
Clare Louise Roberts

I'm a drifter in a dream
But what ya think I'm doing is not all it seems
I may be making coffee nine to five
Yet by six o'clock I'll make the world alive

Part of me thinks who needs career plans
I'll worry about that later, I've got plenty of time and
Part of me thinks I'm only twenty-three
Better start applying for a post-grad degree

I'm a drifter in a dream
But what ya think I'm doing is not all it seems
I may be making coffee nine to five
Yet by six o'clock I'll make the world alive

I may not have the world's most wonderful job
But I've got my health and my parents' garage
I don't want to be forty with no prospects no more
In shared accommodation with a student or four

For while I will work
Unpaid as an intern
Then I won't get paid again
And told to wait my turn

I'm a drifter in a dream
But what ya think I'm doing is not all it seems
I may be making coffee nine to five
Yet by six o'clock I'll make the world alive

I'm a drifter in a dream
But what ya think I'm doing is not all it seems
I may be making coffee nine to five
Yet by six o'clock I make the world alive

Let's make the world alive
Let's make the world alive
Make the world alive
Make the world alive
Make the world alive
Make the world alive
Make the world alive
Let's make the world alive

We live in faded dreams
But what is happening is not all it seems
We live in faded dreams
But what is happening is not all it seems

I'm a drifter in a dream
What's happening is not all it seems
It seems
It seems
It seems

Lullaby

Harry Cartwright-Smith

Hey,
You've had a nice day today
Rest your sleepy head
Maybe we'll save the world tomorrow
But first you gotta sleep in bed

Chorus:
You need to gain more energy
That's how Superman flies
We'll do adventures if we've slept
So rest your tiny eyes

If you can't sleep
Call for me
I promise I'll be there
For you I'll try my hardest yet
To complete any dare

Chorus

If I can't help you sleep at first
Then I will try again
I'll sing this song, verse by verse
Till my message sinks in

Chorus

Go to sleep, your work is done
There's one thing left to do
Rest and I'll be satisfied
There's no work left for you

Breathe In Water
Susan Cartwright-Smith

I feel the shiver of the earth
Through my feet and fingertips
The ripple echo flooding outwards.
My hackles rise,
Sensory attention,
As I revert to animal.
I am less than human,
More than divine,
As blood is diverted
And survival is automatic.
I hear my heartbeat
As autumn aroma transports me
Quietly, privately,
To a time before evolution,
And I breathe in water.

The Night We Almost Said Goodbye

Nicola Reed, Nick Pemberton, John Chambers

When raindrops
Slide slowly down your windowpane
First side by side
Draw apart

Then glide together again
Do you ever stop and think about that day
Half light memories
We caught a seaside train
Same old sunshine same old rain
In the helter skelter of a long gone child
Hiding in the shelter of a turning tide
Even streetlights hung their heads and cried
The night we almost said goodbye

The silence
Breaks you so hard that you feel like the rain
The half light
Whispers memories and secrets

Once again
Just out of reach
I see you turn each corner
Every time I look back
Wherever you go the stars and
Streetlights bow their heads down low
As you pass
And I find myself thinking more and more
With my head in the air and my
Feet and my poor heart on the floor,
Was there a darker time?
The night we almost said goodbye

FIND YOURSELF A KEY...

Artwork
Janette Ostle

True To You
Philip Hewitson

Pick up a pen and write some words
Grab your pencil and do a sketch
You're only ever limited by imagination
All you gotta do is fetch some inspiration

Take a brush and paint a picture
Strum those strings and beat that drum
Thoughts and ideas'll fill your head
There never seems to be enough time to get 'em done to your satisfaction

But that's ok
You can do another draft
Add a bit more paint
And record one more take
That's all part of how you make it
True to you

Write some lines and make a story
Roles come to life within your play
Sometimes you write them and sometimes they write you
Characters come to life and go their own way
Even if you protest!

Blank walls and blank pages
Are just canvasses without any paint
Ideas arrive from somewhere I don't know
Tumbling, and in order they most often ain't
More likely spilling from your head
And on the page they go

Something comes over you
Creativity in little bursts
Ideas will rain down
You've gotta try and catch them
Cos in them lies the magic
Which resides within
All you gotta do
Is be true to you

I think a lot of people see poetry as love poems or sad poems… something about a breakup, something that's more directly evocative than it actually can be… but I think you can find gems in poetry, even if the poem isn't about what you thought it was about, you can derive something meaningful from it. It can be a word, it can be a line, it can be a full stop in the right place that just hits you. Poetry is incredibly powerful, and it doesn't have to be world-changing power… Some authors write about the minutiae of life, the tiny little things that you either enjoy for their own sake or that have a wider metaphorical meaning… But whether it seems small or big, poetry has immense power to it.

- Becca Roberts

CROSS COUNTRY
Tony Hendry

In memoriam Nick Pemberton

Of all those who came for you, I guess
I was the only one to go cross country.
There were blackberries, hips and haws,
come to premature, bruised ripeness
in the wet wake of a summer drought,

and, something I'd never noticed,
the florets of a sturdy wayside flower
mimicking sun rays. What was it,
and how much did the name matter?
Common Fleabane? *Just write it down.*

Wet grass and cowpats in the meadow,
then the Caldew, full of frothing water
after downpours. On the footbridge,
I looked hard for a dipper's white bib
or a kingfisher's cobalt flash. Not today.

Today, the steep lane to Cummersdale
in mizzle, past the scrap metal clutter
where travellers lived. In the neat village,
with Redfern pub and flowers in tyres
on the green, the clouds parted briefly.

I sought rainbows, still hungry for signs.
But the clouds rejoined, and rain came,
and me and my lopsided blue umbrella
battled on to Dalston Road, turned right
past the Pirelli factory, got to the grounds

of the crematorium, and found a bench.
I wiped my shoes, put on my black tie
as clumsily as a kid, and moved towards
the host of people there to honour you,
and you said again *Just write it down.*

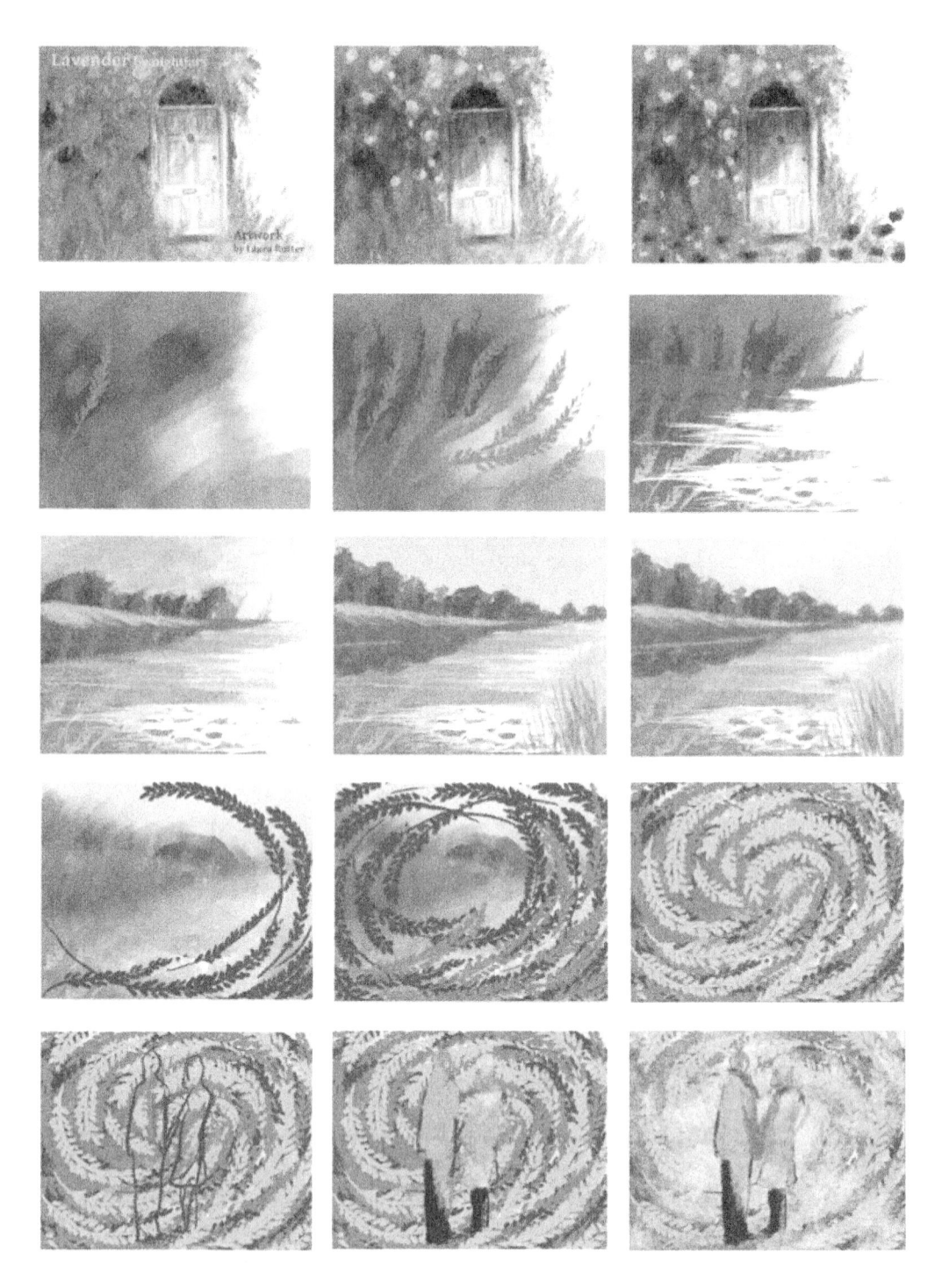

Artwork for 'Lavender'
Laura Rutter

Lavender
Nicola Reed, John Chambers, Andy Hopkins

There was time when roses grew wild around my door
Sweet columbines and poppy blooms danced in silky gowns they wore
But now the wind shakes ravaged leaves impaled on naked thorn
All that is left is lavender to soothe this icy dawn

There was river cool and green, as long as summer days
Where lovers swelled with promises washed by forgetful waves
But now days fly by like spears and the river flows unseen
And all that is left is lavender reminding them to breathe

Oh lavender, sweet lavender, swear we'll never part
For who can sing a sweeter song than lavender to a grieving heart
Don't leave me now
Don't lead me howling through this languid rain
For while there is love and lavender summer will remain,
Where there is love and lavender here I will remain

the mad accordion
Nick Pemberton

Take the box,
shake the box,
if you must
(and you must)
snap the hasp
and break the locks
and take out the mad accordion...

Let your fingers stroke its keys
let its slinky plaintive wheeze
lead you through the darkening trees
to a landing stage upon a lake shore
where reeds creak and dandelion spore
and duck down dance down to the water
where, beneath the silver surface, spiky perch fins glisten
and now - between heartbeats - you pause, and you listen...

This time, hold it close, soon it will be gone
like the secret dreams locked in the heart
of the mad accordion...

So amongst the shadows of the builders'
breezeblock open your shoulders, raise your head,
play the mad squeezebox until you're dead,
until every prodigal daughter, every runaway son
walks home across the windblown water
on a winding stair of thought. Trade each note
for the next note, there are only these, there are no more
and each note that's gone leaves nothing behind,
no stepping stones lead back to the shore.
Squeeze the mad squeezebox, squeeze diamonds to dust
or stretch air into insubstantial chains of melody,
a living entity that still, through stillness, leads you on...

Find yourself a key,
play it, play it,
(as if you were free)
play it, play it,
play it till time bends,
play it, play it,
play it till you lose friends
play it play it
play it till the song ends
play it play it
all alone
play it weary to the bone
play it, play it
play it till your fingers are sore
play it, play it...

Now take a deep breath
and play it some more.

Silver fish, like lightning
play the mad accordion

Nightjars in the shadows
play the mad accordion

The momentum in the breaking waves
plays the mad accordion

The patients in their hospital beds
walk through the trapdoors in their heads
to play the mad accordion

Bugs bunny with his looney tunes
on a million TVs on a million afternoons
still plays the mad accordion

stretch a cage around the sun
with the words of the mad accordion

Play me, play me till I break
or the world is broken and I belong,
play me till each word is spoken
and each spoken word becomes a song

So says

(or maybe prays)

the man who plays the man

who played the man who is played

by

the mad accordion

Stormy Seas
Craig Davidson

Nick Pemberton, Becca Roberts and Kelly Davis read the responses in the group poem on Isolation, Overcoming Isolation and Freedom at 'SpeakEasy' at Foxes Café Lounge on Wednesday 25th April 2018.

Acknowledgements

'Resonance' and 'The Gift' by Josephine Dickinson
With thanks to *Faith in the Moor*, August 2020, (http://www.alstonmoorcofe.org.uk/fitm.html) who published 'Resonance', and to 21 Fragments: Life in the Time of Covid-19 (*A Commonplace Blog* http://acommonplaceblog.com) who published 'The Gift'.

And with thanks to *Ygdrasil: A Journal of the Poetic Arts*, who published these two poems as #11 and #12 of the full sequence *Fragments From an Early Life*.

'Conversation with my father' by Kelly Davis
This poem was selected for https://www.lukejerram.com/breadpoetry/

'Easter Sunday Morning, Wigton, (12 April 2020)' by Janette Ostle
This poem was previously published in Square Wheel Press' *Together & Apart* anthology, and a copy of it is also stored in Barrow Archives.

'Between the Lines' by Barbara Renel
This story appears in *SpeakEasy Magazine: Freiraum* (2018) and *SpeakEasy Magazine Issue No. 2* (2017).

Image of Becca Roberts - page 96
A still taken from the short film *Cross Country* which was filmed, edited and produced by BAFTA award winning cinematographer Keith Partridge.

'Cross Country' by Tony Hendry
This poem appears in *Fresh Air* (2019) published by Caldew Press.

'The Mad Accordion' by Nick Pemberton
Published here by kind permission of Francesca Halfacree and the Pemberton family. Also published in *Eat The Peach* by Tutti Frutti Press in 2021.

QR code links:

Page iv: https://www.youtube.com/watch?v=yQk2meKikKw

Page 4:   https://www.youtube.com/playlist?list=PLPmlQaNGyyOzQ8yrqfQDqNh0ieOgV7wpN

Page 8:   https://www.youtube.com/watch?v=1G7fxFeNB1g

Page 9:   https://www.youtube.com/watch?v=azq9eGKnKQo

Page 11:   https://www.youtube.com/watch?v=c14sqFGYvTc

Page 13:   https://www.youtube.com/watch?v=9ngIe_N4qZU

Page 104:   https://www.youtube.com/watch?v=UCMxwYYSj3E

Biographies

Ally Barr lives near Cockermouth. She writes and scull rows, but not at the same time, or she would probably fall in. She enjoys the simple things in life: gazing up at stars, watching a kingfisher dive, water patterns and reflections. Life never fails to amaze her, and her rollercoaster journey provides an endless supply of wonder and experiences to write about. Coffee and porridge fuel both her pen and her blades. She loves words, nature, science, history, people with empathy, peaceful moments and wild places.

Geoff Bartholomew is a qualified music therapist, working with adults with learning disabilities, older people living with dementia and children with additional support needs.

Harry Cartwright-Smith is an environmental actor and writer. He is part of Extinction Rebellion and has had a story published in Young Writers' Crazy Creatures Northern Capers (2017). He loves to make comics and loads of characters. Some work better than others...

Susan Cartwright-Smith is a tailor (the fabric of fiction, existence and actual cloth), and a wild swimmer and outdoor explorer. She enjoys the freedom of open water, the rhythm of clog dancing and the pattern of gardening. Boys and noise feature prominently in her life. Published in a number of places, including *Cumbria Magazine*, *Forward Poetry*, *Southlight Magazine*, and performed on BBC Radio Cumbria. She is Writer-in-Residence for Cumbria Wildlife Trust's Gosling Sike site and the Solway Coast AONB. She was also part of Caldew Press from 2018 to 2021.

John Chambers has seen angels at Grunne Point, been held at gun point, sings for lost causes, writes because he has to, films because we wants to, and holds the tattered garment of human rights across an increasingly denuded England. He belongs to The Patchwork Opera and is a Nightjrr.

John Charlesworth is an [un]conventional easel painter, employing acrylic paint on canvas or wood. He blends the harsh, unnatural acrylic spectrum to a softer, warmer coloration and tonality, more akin to oils. His subject matter is largely drawn from his imagination, which he feeds continually with observations from the real world. He favours animals for the intriguing shapes they make and as vehicles for ideas and emotions and such. He is an old childhood friend of Nick Pemberton, now living and working in Appleby-in-Westmorland, Cumbria. johncharlesworth.co.uk

Craig Davidson is a former cathedral chorister and amateur rugby league player. ,Craig was born in Carlisle in 1961 and spent most of his working life as a brewery rep. Now semi-retired, he lives in Maryport with his wife and stepchildren, working as a market researcher and enjoying a passion for photography, poetry, Tangerine Dream and Carlisle United F.C.

Kelly Davis was born in London in 1959, and studied English Literature at Oxford University and worked as an editor for Penguin Australia, Longman UK and BBC Books in the 1980s. Since 1989 she and her husband, Ian Francis, have lived in Maryport, West Cumbria. Her poems have been published in *Mslexia*, *The Journal*, *SpeakEasy Magazine*, and anthologised in *Poetry for Performance* (The Playing Space), *Write to be Counted* (The Book Mill), *Diversify* (Fair Acre Press) and *Dusk* (Arachne Press). She is a member of Wigton Writers and the Market Place Poets and chairs sessions at the annual Words by the Water Festival in Keswick, Cumbria.

Josephine Dickinson has published four collections of poetry, including *Silence Fell* (Houghton Mifflin, 2007) and *Night Journey* (Flambard, 2008), and collaborates extensively with artists, musicians and writers. A new collection and a prose memoir are in the pipeline. Active also as a visual artist, Josephine lives on a small hill farm in Alston, Cumbria.

Dr Jane Dudman is an artist, curator and researcher based in Cumbria. She sits on the curatorial panel of the Europe wide Freiraum Platform, which exists to foster cultural and artistic collaboration and action in Europe. She has a research masters and a PhD in Digital Media and Fine Art from Newcastle University. And in addition to her freelance practice is working as a project manager for Prism Arts. Her work is currently sound and performance based with a particular focus on collaborative processes, the spoken word and everyday life. Her artistic research explores the particularity of ordinary experience through sound manipulation and performance strategies, relating the private to the public. She is currently exploring translation, transcription and collective speaking as a form of sense making. Jane has a background in participatory and socially engaged arts practice and has worked in the UK for many years creating and managing arts projects in health, education and community settings. She has directed many live art events, several international artists' exchanges and has shown her work widely in Europe and beyond.

Ros Edwards was born and grew up in Cumbria. She has recently returned. Hopefully not to die, yet, but to enjoy the beauty this area has to offer.

Linda Fitzgerald is an artist and a teacher. 'I completed my Masters Degree in Fine Art in 2011 and since then have developed a Socially Engaged Art practice covering a broad range of interests. I work in photography, text, film and installation. I'm based in Carlisle and I've been working on the Frieraum project with Syrian refugees in Cumbria since April 2018, mainly in collaboration with Kurdish/Syrian, Shireen Hama. At the present time, Shireen and I are developing work with the Lake District Holocaust Project, based in Windermere. They look after the legacy of 300 Jewish orphans based there after the Second World War.'

Juliet Fossey is happiest working outside. Juliet uses nature as a foil for the themes in her work. She likes to work with others as well as alone, collaborating with musicians and artists to produce poetry and spoken word.

Shireen Hama 'I'm a Kurdish refugee from Amouda, Syria, and I'm 22 years old. I have a big family, my mother and seven brothers. We moved to Erbil, Kurdistan because life in Syria became very hard. I couldn't complete my studies so I worked as a volunteer with the Public Aid Organization. I met other refugees and we shared stories. My father died in 2016. It was one of the most difficult moments of my life. Then I came to England in April 2018. It was a very difficult period. Now we are settled in Carlisle and everything is different. Last year I completed an Apprenticeship in Customer Services, and I have successfully resumed my education. This summer I will finish my Access to Art and Design Course and I am now applying for university.'

Tony Hendry was brought up in Cumbria and came back after a Civil Service career in London. Tony returned to writing after a long gap. He had written hundreds of poems in the last few years, and always hoped they were getting better. His pamphlet *Fresh Air* was published by Caldew Press in 2019. Sadly Tony passed away in January 2022 leaving behind a legacy of wonderful poetry.

Philip Hewitson is a writer, poet, illustrator, graphic designer and filmmaker born and raised in Carlisle. He makes films for Tolivar Productions, publishes books as Caldew Press, and hosts SpeakEasy spoken word open mic nights.

Andy Hopkins has taught in London and Carlisle. His chapbooks include *Dark Horse Pictures* (Selkirk Lapwing Press, 2007). His work has appeared in *The North*, *The Interpreter's House*, *Under the Radar*, *Reliquiae*, *Right Hand Pointing*, *Prick of the Spindle*, *Detritus Online* and *Southlight*. A 12" vinyl single (with the band 'nightjrrs') is available from Matchbox Classics Records. He is organiser of the Carlisle Poetry Symposium (@CarlislePoetry) - see https://andyhopkinspoet.wordpress.com for information.

"Sir" Stephen J. C. Hymers is a mad-cap writer, artist and all-round good egg. He has been writing his so-called "Tall Tales & Scary Stories" for some time now. Now 50 years of age, he has said he won't stop writing them! Has such stories as "The Hammond's Pond Horror", "The Swearing Tree" & "The Ghosts of Old Kangol's Lane" published. He claims he writes better after 3 bottles of Pemberton's No.7 Vintage 1979!

Jilly Jarman is Creative Director of BlueJam Arts and runs Improv Choirs, jazz programmes and songwriting projects.

Valerie Moody is a retired civil servant who enjoys writing poetry and teenage fiction. She grew up on the edge of the Lake District and later moved to the West Cumbrian coast, finding much of her inspiration in the stunning scenery that has surrounded her all of her life.

Ben Naga has lived in England all his life, apart from brief periods in France, India and Scotland. Music is probably his greatest love, with England's Lake District not far behind. Lacking the discipline or concentration to write a novel, or even a short story, he prefers to write poetry or lyrics. He was first published in 1968 and examples of his work appeared in two anthologies in the 1970s when he also performed publicly. In the follow two and a half decades he wrote very little, but from 2005 he has returned to writing and performing and currently maintains two websites. He has privately shared Northern Limericks and is working on two books. His poems have been published by a number of online magazines.

Kevin O'Connor has a long career in the arts; training in graphic design, he moved towards fine art painting in the 1970s and has worked in performance art and sculpture. His interest in poetry has developed over the past year along with his launching of an art-based project to promote new collaborative works involving poetry, performance, music and digital media.

Janette Ostle lives and works in Wigton, Cumbria. In her spare time she enjoys reading, writing, drawing/painting, listening to music and going on a good walk. She often finds inspiration from random thoughts which occur whilst taking part in these activities. Prone to occasional tongue-tied moments, she sometimes finds expressing herself on paper easier, as well as cathartic. She believes freedom and space are very important for creativity and creativity can bring positive change.

James Ovens is an artist, illustrator and enthused creative. 'I work in many directions, breathing the efforts of our wonderful humanity despite the cold and weak that linger. I strive for conviction in a sense of seriously asking the question of what am I actually conveying.'

Jill Pemberton studied Fine Art at Brighton, earned an MA in Manchester Met and taught at the University of Cumbria until 2009. She is a member of Green Door Studios and works in acrylics and inks in her studio in Kendal. Her work is loosely abstract unless she gets an urge to draw her cat, who, being old, sits very still.

Nick Pemberton taught creative writing at Cumbria Institute of the Arts, hosted SpeakEasy at different venues in Carlisle for years, starting in 2004 at The Source. He did what The Men in the Smoky Back Room told him to do. He is missed by many. His collection *Eat The Peach* was compiled by Francesca Halfacree and published by Tutti Frutti Press in 2021.

Chris Reed 'My background is in experiential education and the arts therapies. Living and working in Cumbria, I am interested in the arts as a way to explore and express personal experience. I love the way poetry gives words choices, and allows them to be something, to be read on a page, or delivered as performance.'

Nicola Reed 'I have been a singer-songwriter forever and only recently had the courage to start reading poetry without hiding behind a guitar!'

Barbara Renel is a flash fiction writer, mother, dancer, teacher, performer, collaborator, lover of textiles. Her work has appeared in print and online including *Zeroflash*, *Flash Fiction Festival Anthology*, *Flash: The International Short-Story Magazine*, *Spelk*, *Flash-Flood Journal*, theshotstory.co.uk, *Structo*, *A3 Review*. She has an MA in Creative Writing from Lancaster University, where she specialised in the short story form. Twitter: @barbara_renel. Website: www.postcard-stories.uk

Carolyn Patricia Richardson is a poet, a painter with work in the Public Catalogue, now re-branded as ArtUK, a maker of filmed poems and a guerrilla poet in the wilds of Dumfries & Galloway. Carolyn was a Director of the Scottish Writers Centre & her filmpoem "Spring Train" was commended in Cumbria's FilmFling in 2017. She is widely published through writing articles for journals & by regularly contributing poems and filmpoems. Carolyn is happy to create films based on your poems so contact her at poempics@icloud.com. She is published by Red Squirrel Press, who published her book *Scots' Rock* in 2016 (www.redsquirrelpress.com). Among her various creative initiatives, Carolyn has worked as an advisor for the Creative Industries Sector of the Dumfries & Galloway Chamber of Commerce (www.dgchamber.co.uk). Carolyn is lucky enough to spend some of the year abroad writing and painting in the South of France in the National Booktown of Montolieu (www.montolieu-livre.fr).

James Scott Riddick is a poet and performer of sorts. His work has appeared in *The Cadavarine*, *SpeakEasy Magazine* and on BBC Radio Cumbria, where he uneasily occupies the role of resident poet. He was also a founding member of the group Working Class Artists, who can be found under that name on the relevant channels.

Becca Roberts was born in Liverpool, raised in Belfast and lives in Carlisle. Her accent is, understandably, confused. She graduated with a BA in Performing Arts in 2008, and she is now a professional proofreader. Becca performs other people's poetry at the longstanding SpeakEasy open-mic night and other performance events, and she is part of a local theatre group. When not in the mood for literary pursuits, she enjoys bouldering, both indoors and on various slabs of rock around Cumbria, as well as ploughing, planting and picking at her allotment (plus pickling and preserving the produce). She also enjoys alliteration.

Clare Louise Roberts a.k.a. Little Strings is a Welsh musician and writer living in Glasgow, playing indie/folk/pop music on the ukulele. She likes to write plays about social media and songs about her Netflix bingeing habits. She has a personal essay published in the 3rd issue of the *BODIES* zine and satirical pieces for online magazine *Quaranzine*. She released new music – some pretty, some ridiculous – in 2021.

Marc Robinson is a local Cumbrian artist who specialises in acrylic landscapes and pen and ink work. Marc had a successful solo exhibition at Carlisle's Old Fire Station in 2019. He also writes and illustrates his own books. The paintings submitted for this book illustrate the feelings of isolation and hope during lockdown.

Peter Robinson lived in Carlisle and was inspired to write his poem during the first lockdown in the COVID-19 pandemic in 2020. Peter sadly passed away suddenly in 2021.

Lou Rodger is many things; writer, artist, potter to name just three! A regular contributor to Poets Out Loud, Lou tries to make it to SpeakEasy whenever possible. Now shaping young minds through teacher training, Lou is a passionate Climate Change campaigner and has organised several climate strikes in Cockermouth.

Laura Rutter is an illustrator by training who works using watercolour and various digital mediums. Her creative practice focuses on showcasing the process of how a piece is created, and the exploratory thought process of the artist.

David Simmons Writing his first haiku in December 2018, it took him 62 years to progress from "ga ga" to "gaga ooh la la". Attempting to document "hidden Carlisle" and 40 years' love for the city, writing haiku onto white cotton tape transformed the project into a simple art form of natural energy. Contributing to Carlisle Unity festival, Mind Trees of the Urban Forest and The Gate exhibitions and as a solo installation draping Bitts Park pagoda for 3 days in August, the exhibition "Carlisle in Haiku form" graced the south aisle of Carlisle Cathedral for 13 days in October 2019. His book *Carlisle in Haiku Form: First Impressions* was published by Caldew Press in 2021.

Fernando Smith is the performing name for Mark Griffiths, an artist, poet, singer and performer living in Cumbria. He has performed his work to audiences across the country and Europe. His work has appeared in journals, pamphlets and publications, including the *Best of Manchester Poets Volume 1* and *2*, *Abridged: Desire and Dust* (Arts Council of Northern Ireland) and *Words for Wellbeing* (NHS Foundation Publishing). His first collection of poetry *Welcome to the Golden Life* was published in 2010 and Caldew Press published *GRID* in 2021. www.fernandosmith.co.uk

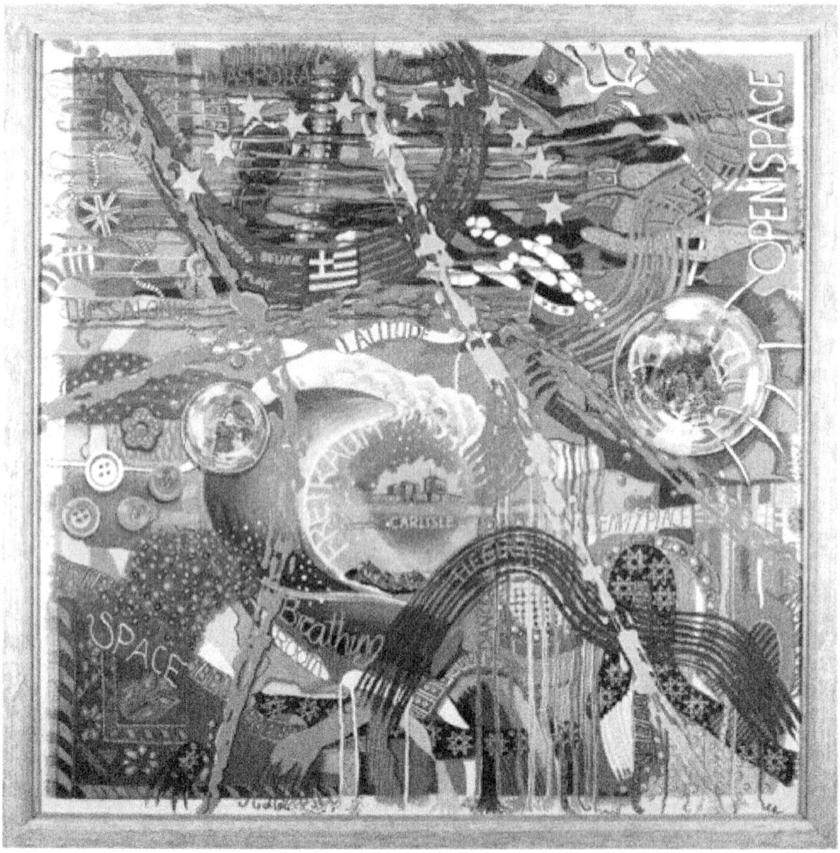
DIASPORA
OPEN SPACE
LATITUDE
CARLISLE
SPACE
Breathing

Printed in Great Britain
by Amazon